CHARLES H. SPURGEON

THE
HOLY SPIRIT
How to be filled with the Holy Spirit

TABLE OF CONTENTS

Chapter 1. The Personality of the Holy Ghost----------------------------------3
Chapter 2. The Holy Spirit's Chief Office------------------------------------16
Chapter 3. The Holy Spirit Glorifying Christ--------------------------------31
Chapter 4. The Work of the Holy Spirit--------------------------------------46
Chapter 5. The Necessity of the Spirit's Work-------------------------------58
Chapter 6. The Holy Spirit's Intercession-----------------------------------71
Chapter 7. Adoption—The Spirit and the Cry----------------------------------86
Chapter 8. Grieving the Holy Spirit---101
Chapter 9. The Holy Spirit and the One Church------------------------------115
Chapter 10. The Power of the Holy Ghost------------------------------------127
Chapter 11. The Outpouring of the Holy Spirit------------------------------141

Chapter 1
THE PERSONALITY OF THE HOLY GHOST

"And I will pray the Father, and he shall give you another Comforter, that he may abide with you for ever; even the Spirit of truth; whom the world cannot receive, because it seeth him not, neither knoweth him: but ye know him; for he dwelleth with you, and shall be in you."—John 14:16-17

You will be surprised to hear me announce that I do not intend this morning to say anything about the Holy Spirit as the Comforter. I propose to reserve that for a special Sermon this evening. In this discourse I shall endeavor to explain and enforce certain other doctrines, which I believe are plainly taught in this text, and which I hope God the Holy Ghost may make profitable to our souls. Old John Newton once said, that there were some books which he could not read;—they were good and sound enough; but, said he, "they are books of halfpence;—you have to take so much in quantity before you have any value; there are other books of silver, and others of gold; but I have one book that is a book of bank notes; and every leaf is a bank-note of immense value." So I found with this text: that I had a bank-note of so large a sum, that I could not tell it out all this morning. I should have to keep you several hours before I could unfold to you the whole value of this precious promise—one of the last which Christ gave his people.

I invite your attention to this passage because we shall find in it some instruction on four points: first, concerning the true and proper personality of the Holy Ghost; secondly, concerning the united agency of the glorious Three Persons in the work of our salvation; thirdly we shall find something to establish the doctrine of the indwelling of the Holy Ghost in the souls of all believers; and fourthly, we shall find out the reason why the carnal mind rejects the Holy Ghost.

I. First of all, we shall have some little instruction concerning the proper personality of the Holy Spirit. We are so much accustomed to talk about the influence of the Holy Ghost and his sacred operations and graces, that we are apt to forget that the Holy Spirit is truly and actually a person—that he is a subsistence—an existence; or, as we Trinitarians usually say, one person in the essence of the Godhead. I am afraid that, though we do not know it, we have acquired the habit of regarding the Holy Ghost as an emanation flowing from the Father and the Son, but not as being actually a person himself. I know it is not easy to carry about in our mind the idea of the Holy Spirit as a person. I can think of the Father as a person, because his acts are such as I can understand. I see him hang the world in ether; I behold him swaddling a new-born sea in bands of darkness; I know it is he who formed the drops of hail, who leadeth forth the stars by their hosts, and calleth them by their name; I can conceive of Him as a person, because I behold his operations. I can realize Jesus, the Son of Man, as a real person, because he is bone of my bone and flesh of my flesh. It takes no great stretch of my imagination to picture the babe in Bethlehem, or to behold the "Man of sorrows and acquainted with grief," of the king of martyrs, as he was persecuted in Pilate's hall, or nailed to the accursed tree for our sins. Nor do I find it difficult at times to realize the person of my Jesus sitting on his throne in heaven; or girt with clouds and wearing the diadem of all creation, calling the earth to judgment, and summoning us to hear our final sentence. But when I come to deal with the Holy Ghost, his operations are so mysterious, his doings are so secret, his acts are so removed from everything that is of sense, and of the body, that I cannot so easily get the idea of his being a person; but a person he is. God the Holy Ghost is not an influence, an emanation, a stream of something flowing from the Father; but he is as much an actual person as either God the Son, or God the Father. I shall attempt this morning a little to establish the doctrine, and to show you the truth of it—that God the Holy Spirit is actually a person.

    The first proof we shall gather from the pool of holy baptism. Let me take you down, as I have taken others, into the pool, now concealed, but which I wish were always open to your view. Let me take you to the baptismal font, where believers put on the name of the Lord Jesus, and you shall hear me pronounce the solemn words, "I baptize thee in the name,"—mark, "in the name," not names—"of the Father, and of the Son, and of the Holy Ghost." Every one who is baptized according to the true form laid down in Scripture, must be a Trinitarian: otherwise his baptism is a farce and a lie, and he himself is found a deceiver and a hypocrite before God. As the Father is mentioned, and as the Son is mentioned, so is the Holy Ghost; and the whole is summed up as being a Trinity in unity, by its being said, not the names, but the "name" the glorious name, the Jehovah name, "of the Father, and of the Son, and of the Holy Ghost." Let me remind you that the same thing occurs each time you are dismissed from this house of prayer. In pronouncing the solemn closing benediction, we invoke on your behalf the love of Jesus Christ, the grace of the Father, and the fellowship of the Holy Spirit; and thus, according to the apostolic manner, we make a manifest distinction between the persons, showing that we believe the Father to be a person, the Son to be a person, and the Holy Ghost to be a person. Were there no other proofs in Scripture, I think these would be sufficient for every sensible man. He would see that if the Holy Spirit were a mere influence, he would not be mentioned in conjunction with two whom we all confess to be actual and proper persons.

A second argument arises from the fact that the Holy Ghost has actually made different appearances on earth. The Great Spirit has manifested himself to man: he has put on a form, so that, whilst he has not been beheld by mortal men, he has been so veiled in appearance that he was seen, so far as that appearance was concerned, by the eyes of all beholders. See you Jesus Christ our Saviour? There is the river Jordan, with its shelving banks and its willows weeping at its side. Jesus Christ, the Son of God, descends into the stream, and the holy Baptist, John, plunges him into the waves. The doors of heaven are opened; a miraculous appearance presents itself; a bright light shineth from the sky, brighter than the sun in all its grandeur, and down in a flood of glory descends something which you recognize to be a dove. It rests on Jesus—it sits upon his sacred head, and as the old painters put a halo round the brow of Jesus, so did the Holy Ghost shed a resplendence around the face of him who came to fulfil all righteousness, and therefore commenced with the ordinance of baptism. The Holy Ghost was seen as a dove, to mark his purity and his gentleness, and he came down like a dove from heaven to show that it is from heaven alone that he descendeth. Nor is this the only time when the Holy Ghost has been manifest in a visible shape. You see that company of disciples gathered together in an upper room; they are waiting for some promised blessing, and bye-and-bye it shall come. Hark! there is a sound as of a rushing mighty wind; it fills all the house where they are sitting; and astonished, they look around them, wondering what will come next. Soon a bright light appears, shining upon the heads of each: cloven tongues of fire sat upon them. What were these marvelous appearances of wind and flame but a display of the Holy Ghost in his proper person? I say the fact of an appearance manifests that he must be a person. An influence could not appear—an attribute could not appear: we cannot see attributes—we cannot behold influences. The Holy Ghost must, then, have been a person; since he was beheld by mortal eyes, and he came under the cognizance of mortal sense.

Another proof is from the fact, that personal qualities are, in Scripture, ascribed to the Holy Ghost. First, let me read to you a text in which the Holy Ghost is spoken of as having understanding. In the 1st Epistle to the Corinthians, chap. ii., you will read, "But as it is written, eye hath not seen, nor ear heard, neither hath it entered into the heart of man, the things which God hath prepare for them that love him. But God have revealed them unto us by his Spirit: for the Spirit searcheth all things, yea, the deep things of God. For what man knoweth the things of a man, save the spirit of man which is in him? Even so the things of God knoweth no man, but the Spirit of God." Here you see an understanding—a power of knowledge is ascribed to the Holy Ghost. Now, if there be any persons here whose minds are of so preposterous a complexion that they would ascribe one attribute to another, and would speak of a mere influence having understanding, then I give up all the argument. But I believe every rational man will admit, that when anything is spoken of as having an understanding, it must be an existence—it must, in fact, be a person. In the 12th chap., 11th verse of the same Epistle, you will find a will ascribed to the Holy Spirit. "But all these worketh that one and the self-same spirit, dividing to every man severally as he will." So it is plain that the Spirit has a will. He does not come from God simply at God's will, but he has a will of his own, which is always in keeping with the will of the infinite Jehovah, but is, nevertheless, distinct and separate; therefore, I say he is a person. In another text, power is ascribed to the Holy Ghost, and power is a thing which can only be ascribed to an existence. In Romans 15:13, it is written, "Now the God of hope fill you with all joy and peace in believing, that ye may abound in hope through the power of the Holy Ghost." I need not insist upon it, because it is self-evident, that wherever you find understanding, will, and power, you must also find an existence; it cannot be a mere attribute, it cannot be a metaphor, it cannot be a personified influence; but it must be a person.

But I have a proof which, perhaps, will be more telling upon you than any other. Acts and deeds are ascribed to the Holy Ghost; therefore, he must be a person. You read in the first chapter of the Book of Genesis, that the Spirit brooded over the surface of the earth, when it was as yet all disorder and confusion. This world was once a mass of chaotic matter, there was no order; it was like the valley of darkness and of the shadow of death. God the Holy Ghost spread his wings over it; he sowed the seeds of life in it; the germs from which all beings sprang were implanted by him; he impregnated the earth so that it became capable of life. Now, it must have been a person who brought order out of confusion: it must have been an existence who hovered over this world and made it what it now is. But do we not read in Scripture something more of the Holy Ghost? Yes, we are told that "holy men of old spake as they were moved by the Holy Ghost." When Moses penned the Pentateuch, the Holy Ghost moved his hand; when David wrote the Psalms, and discoursed sweet music on his harp, it was the Holy Spirit that gave his fingers their seraphic motion; when Solomon dropped from his lips the words of the proverbs of wisdom, or when he hymned the Canticles of love, it was the Holy Ghost who gave him words of knowledge and hymns of rapture. Ah! and what fire was that which touched the lips of the eloquent Isaiah? What hand was that which came upon Daniel? What might was that which made Jeremiah so plaintive in his grief? or what was that which winged Ezekiel and made him like an eagle, soar into mysteries aloft, and see the mighty unknown beyond our reach? Who was it that made Amos, the herdsman, a prophet? Who taught the rugged Haggai to pronounce his thundering sentences? Who showed Habakkuk the horses of Jehovah marching through the waters? or who kindled the burning eloquence of Nahum? Who caused Malachi to close up the book with the muttering of the word curse? Who was it in each of these, save the Holy Ghost? And must it not have been a person who spake in and through these ancient witnesses? We must believe it. We cannot avoid believing it, when we read that "holy men of old spake as they were moved by the Holy Ghost."

And when has the Holy Ghost ceased to have an influence upon men? We find that still he deals with his ministers and with all his saints. Turn to the Acts, and you will find that the Holy Ghost said, "Separate me Paul and Barnabas for the work." I never heard of an attribute saying such a thing. The Holy Spirit said to Peter, "Go to the Centurion, and what I have cleansed, that call not thou common." The Holy Ghost caught away Philip after he had baptized the Eunuch, and carried him away to another place; and the Holy Ghost said to Paul; "Thou shalt not go into that city, but shall turn into another." And we know that the Holy Ghost was lied unto by Ananias and

Sapphira, when it was said, "Thou hast not lied unto man, but unto God." Again, that power which we feel every day, who are called to preach—that wondrous spell which makes our lips so potent—that power which gives us thoughts which are like birds from a far-off region, not the natives of our soul—that influence which I sometimes strangely feel, which, if it does not give me poetry and eloquence, gives me a might I never felt before, and lifts me above my fellow-man—that majesty with which he clothes his ministers, till in the midst of the battle they cry aha! like the war-horse of Job, and move themselves like leviathans in the water—that power which gives us might over men, and causes them to sit and listen as if their ears were chained, as if they were entranced by the power of some magician's wand—that power must come from a person; it must come from the Holy Ghost.

But is it not said in Scripture, and do we not feel it, dear brethren, that it is the Holy Ghost who regenerates the soul? It is the Holy Ghost who quickens us. "You hath he quickened who were dead in trespasses and sins." It is the Holy Spirit who imparts the first germ of life, convincing us of sin, of righteousness, and of judgment to come. And is it not the Holy Spirit, who, after that flame is kindled, still fans it with the breath of his mouth and keeps it alive? Its author is its preserver. Oh! can it be said that it is the Holy Ghost who strives in men's souls; that it is the Holy Ghost who brings them into the sweet place that is called Calvary—can it be said that he does all these things, and yet is not a person? It may be said, but it must be said by fools; for he never can be a wise man who can consider these things can be done by any other than a glorious person—a divine existence.

Allow me to give you one more proof, and I shall have done. Certain feelings are ascribed to the Holy Ghost, which can only be understood upon the supposition that he is actually a person. In the 4th chapter of Ephesians, v. 30, it is said that the Holy Ghost can be grieved: "Grieve not the Holy Spirit of God, whereby ye are sealed unto the day of redemption." In Isaiah, chap. lxiii, v. 10, it is said that the Holy Ghost can be vexed: "But they rebelled, and vexed his Holy Spirit; therefore he was turned to be their enemy., and he fought against them." In Acts, chap. vii. v. 51, you read that the Holy Ghost can be resisted: "Ye stiff-necked and uncircumcised in heart and ears, ye do always resist the Holy Ghost; as your fathers did, so do ye." And in the 5th chapter, v. 9, of the same book, you will find that the Holy Ghost may be tempted. We are informed that Peter said to Ananias and Sapphira, "How is it that ye have agreed together to tempt the Spirit of the

Lord?" Now, these things could not be emotions which might be ascribed to a quality or an emanation; they must be understood to relate to a person; an influence could not be grieved, it must be a person who can be grieved, vexed, or resisted.

And now, dear brethren, I think I have fully established the point of the personality of the Holy Ghost; allow me now, most earnestly, to impress upon you the absolute necessity of being sound on the doctrine of the Trinity. I knew a man, a good minister of Jesus Christ he is now, and I believe he was before he turned his eyes unto heresy—he began to doubt the glorious divinity of our blessed Lord, and for years did he preach the heterodox doctrine, until one day he happened to hear a very eccentric old minister preaching from the text, "But there the glorious Lord shall be unto us a place of broad rivers and streams, wherein shall go no galley with oars, neither shall gallant ship pass thereby. Thy tacklings are loosed; they could not well strengthen their mast, they could not spread the sail." "Now," said the old minister, "you give up the Trinity, and your tacklings are loosed, you cannot strengthen your masts. Once give up the doctrine of three persons, and your tacklings are all gone; your mast, which ought to be a support to your vessel, is a rickety one, and shakes." A gospel without the Trinity! it is a pyramid built upon its apex. A gospel without the Trinity! it is a rope of sand that cannot hold together. A gospel without the Trinity! then, indeed, Satan can overturn it. But give me a gospel with the Trinity, and the might of hell cannot prevail against it; no man can any more overthrow it than a bubble could split a rock, or a feather break in halves a mountain. Get the thought of the three persons, and you have the marrow of all divinity. Only know the Father, and know the Son, and know the Holy Ghost to be one, and all things will appear clear. This is the golden key to the secrets of nature; this is the silken clue of the labyrinths of mystery, and he who understands this, will soon understand as much as mortals e'er can know.

II. Now for our second point—the united agency of the three persons in the work of our salvation. Look at the text, and you will find all the three persons mentioned. "I"—that is the Son—"will pray the Father, and he shall give you another Comforter." There are the three persons mentioned, all of them doing something for our salvation. "I will pray," says the Son. "I will send," says the Father. "I will comfort," says the Holy Ghost. now, let us, for a few moments, discourse upon this wondrous theme—the unity of the three persons with regard to the great purpose of the salvation of the elect. When

God first made man, he said, "Let us make man," not let me, but, "Let us make man in our own image." The covenant Elohim said to each other, "Let us unitedly become the creator of man." So, when in ages far gone by, in eternity, they said, "Let us save man:" it was not the Father who said, "Let me save man, "but the three persons conjointly said, with one consent, "Let us save man." It is to me a source of sweet comfort to think that it is not one person of the Trinity that is engaged for my salvation; it is not simply one person of the Godhead who vows that he will redeem me; but it is a glorious trio of Godlike ones, and the three declare, unitedly, "We will save man."

Now, observe here, that each person is spoken of as performing a separate office. "I will pray," says the Son; that is intercession. "I will send," says the Father; that is donation. "I will comfort," says the Holy Spirit; that is supernatural influence. O! if it were possible for us to see the three persons of the Godhead, we should behold one of them standing before the throne, with outstretched hands, crying day and night, "O, Lord, how long?" We should see one girt with Urim and Thummim, precious stones, on which are written the twelve names of the tribes of Israel; we should behold him, crying unto his Father, "Forget not thy promises, forget not thy covenant;" we should hear him make mention of our sorrows, and tell forth our griefs on our behalf, for he is our intercessor. And could we behold the Father, we should not see him a listless and idle spectator of the intercession of the Son, but we should see him with attentive ear listening to every word of Jesus, and granting every petition. Where is the Holy Spirit all the while? Is he lying idle? O no; he is floating over the earth, and when he seas a weary soul, he says, "Come to Jesus, he will give you rest;" when he beholds an eye filled with tears, he wipes away the tears, and bids the mourner look for comfort on the cross; when he sees the tempest-tossed believer, he takes the helm of his soul and speaks the word of consolation; he helpeth the broken in heart, and bindeth up their wounds; and, ever on his mission of mercy, he flies around the world, being everywhere present. Behold, how the three persons work together. Do not then say, "I am grateful to the Son"—so you ought to be, but God the Son no more saves you than God the Father. Do not imagine that God the Father is a great tyrant, and that God the Son had to die to make him merciful. It was not to make the Father's love towards his people. Oh, no. One loves as much as the other; the three are conjoined in the great purpose of rescuing the elect from damnation.

But you must notice another thing in my text, which will show the blessed unity of the three—the one person promises to the other. The Son says, "I will pray the Father." "Very well," the disciples may have said, "we can trust you for that." "And he will send you." You see, here is the Son signing a bond on behalf of the Father. "He will send you another Comforter." There is a bond on behalf of the Holy Spirit too. "And he will abide with you forever." One person speaks for the other, and how could they, if there were any disagreement between them? If one wished to save, and the other not, they could not promise on another's behalf. But whatever the Son says, the Father listens to; whatever the Father promises, the Holy Ghost works; and, whatever the Holy Ghost injects into the soul, that God the Father fulfils. So, the three together mutually promise on one another's behalf. There is a bond with three names appended—Father, Son, and Holy Ghost. By three immutable things, as well as by two, the Christian is secured beyond the reach of death and hell. A Trinity of securities, because there is a Trinity of God.

III, Our third point is, the indwelling of the Holy Ghost in believers. Now, beloved, these first two things have been matters of pure doctrine; this is the subject of experience. The indwelling of the Holy Ghost is a subject so profound, and so having to do with the inner man, that no soul will be able truly and really to comprehend what I say, unless it has been taught of God. I have heard of an old minister, who told a fellow of one of the Cambridge colleges, that he understood a language that he never learned in all his life. "I have not," he said, "even a smattering of Greek, and I know no Latin, but thank God, I can talk the language of Canaan, and that is more than you can." So, beloved, I shall now have to talk a little of the language of Canaan. If you cannot comprehend me, I am much afraid it is because you are not of Israelitish extraction; you are not a child of God, nor an inheritor of the kingdom of heaven.

We are told in the text, that Jesus would send the Comforter, who would abide in the saints forever; who would dwell with them, and be in them. Old Ignatius, the martyr, used to call himself Theophorus, or Godbearer, "because," said he, "I bear about with me the Holy Ghost." And truly every Christian is a Godbearer. "Know ye not that ye are the temples of the Holy Ghost? for he dwelleth in you?" That man is no Christian who is not the subject of the indwelling of the Holy Spirit; he may talk well, he may understand theology, and be a sound Calvinist; he will be the child of nature finely dressed, but not the living child. He may be a man of so profound an intellect, so gigantic a soul, so comprehensive a mind, and so lofty an imagination, that he may dive into all the secrets of nature, may know the path which the eagle's eye hath not seen, and go into depths where the ken of mortals reacheth not, but he shall not be a Christian with all his knowledge, he shall not be a son of God with all his researches, unless he understands what it is to have the Holy Ghost dwelling in him and abiding in him; yea, and that for ever.

Some people call this fanaticism, and they say, "You are a Quaker; why not follow George Fox?" Well, we would not mind that much: we would follow any one who followed the Holy Ghost. Even he, with all his eccentricities, I doubt not, was, in many cases, actually inspired by the Holy Spirit; and whenever I find a man in whom there rests the Spirit of God, the spirit within me leaps to hear the spirit within him, and we feel that we are one. The Spirit of God in one Christian soul recognizes the Spirit in another. I recollect talking with a good man, as I believe he was, who was insisting that it was impossible for us to know whether we had the Holy Spirit within us or not. I should like him to be here this morning, because I would read this verse to him, "But ye know him, for he dwelleth with you, and shall be in you." Ah! you think you cannot tell whether you have the Holy Spirit or not. Can I tell whether I am alive or not? If I were touched by electricity, could I tell whether I was or not? I suppose I should; the shock would be strong enough to make me know where I stood. So, if I have God within me —if I have Deity tabernacling in my breast—if I have God the Holy Ghost resting in my heart, and making a temple of my body, do you think I shall know it? Call it fanaticism if you will, but I trust that there are some of us who know what it is to be always, or generally, under the influence of the Holy Spirit—always in one sense, generally in another. When we have difficulties, we ask the direction of the Holy Ghost. When we do not understand a portion of Holy Scripture, we ask God the Holy Ghost to shine upon us. When we are depressed, the Holy Ghost comforts us. You cannot tell what the wondrous power of the indwelling of the Holy Ghost is; how it pulls back the hand of the saint when he would touch the forbidden thing; how it prompts him to make a covenant with his eyes; how it binds his feet, lest they should fall in a slippery way; how it restrains his heart, and keeps him from temptation. O ye, who know nothing of the indwelling of the Holy Ghost, despise it not. O despise not the Holy Ghost, for it is the unpardonable sin. "He that speaketh a word against the Son of Man, it shall be forgiven him, but he that speaketh against the Holy Ghost, it shall never be forgiven him, either in this life, or that which is to come." So saith the Word of God. Therefore tremble, lest in anything ye despise the influences of the Holy Spirit.

But before closing this point, there is one little word that pleases me very much, that is "forever." You knew I should not miss that; you were certain I could not let it go without observation. "Abide with you forever." I wish I could get an Armenian here to finish my sermon. I fancy I see him taking that word "forever." He would say, "for—forever;" he would have to stammer and stutter; for he could never get it out all at once. He might stand and pull it about, and at last he would have to say, "The translation is wrong." And I suppose the poor man would have to prove that the original was wrong too. Ah! but blessed be God we can read it—"He shall abide with you forever." Once give me the Holy Ghost, and I shall never lose him till "forever" has run out; till eternity has spun its everlasting rounds.

IV. Now we have to close up with a brief remark on the reason why the world rejects the Holy Ghost. It is said, "Whom the world cannot receive, because it seeth him not, neither knoweth him." You know what is sometimes meant by "the world"—those whom God in his wondrous sovereignty passed over when he chose his people: the preterite ones; those passed over in God's wondrous preterition—not the reprobates who were condemned to damnation by some awful decree; but those passed over by God, when he chose out his elect. These cannot receive the Spirit. Again, it means all in a carnal state are not able to procure themselves this divine influence; and, thus it is true, "Whom the world cannot receive."

The unregenerate world of sinners despises the Holy Ghost, "because it seeth him not." Yes, I believe this is the great secret why many laugh at the idea of the existence of the Holy Ghost—because they see him not. You tell the worldling, "I have the Holy Ghost within me." He says, "I cannot see it." He wants it to be something tangible—a thing he can recognize with his senses. Have you ever heard the argument used by a good old Christian against an infidel doctor? The doctor said there was no soul, and asked, "Did you ever see a soul?" "No," said the Christian. "Did you ever hear a soul?" "No." "Did you ever smell a soul?" "No." "Did you ever taste a soul?" "No." "Did you ever feel a soul?" "Yes," said the man—"I feel I have one within me." "Well," said the doctor, "there are four senses against one; you only have one on your side." "Very well," said the Christian, "Did you ever see a

13

pain?" "No." "Did you ever hear a pain?" "No." "Did you ever smell a pain?" "No." "Did you ever taste a pain?" "No." "Did you ever feel a pain?" "Yes." "And that is quite enough, I suppose, to prove there is a pain?" "Yes." So the worldling says there is no Holy Ghost, because he cannot see it. Well, but we feel it. You say that is fanaticism, and that we never felt it. Suppose you tell me that honey is bitter, I reply, "No, I am sure you cannot have tasted it; taste it and try." So with the Holy Ghost; if you did but feel his influence, you would no longer say there is no Holy Spirit, because you cannot see it. Are there not many things, even in nature, which we cannot see? Did you ever see the wind? No; but ye know there is wind, when you behold the hurricane tossing the waves about, and rending down the habitations of men; or when, in the soft evening zephyr, it kisses the flowers, and maketh dew-drops hang in pearly coronets around the rose. Did ye ever see electricity? No; but ye know there is such a thing, for it travels along the wires for thousands of miles, and carries our messages; though you cannot see the thing itself, you know there is such a thing. So you must believe there is a Holy Ghost working in us, both to will and to do, even though it is beyond our senses.

But the last reason why worldly men laugh at the doctrine of the Holy Spirit, is, because they do not know it. If they know it by heartfelt experience and if they recognized its agency in the soul; if they had ever been touched by it; if they had been made to tremble under a sense of sin; if they had had their hearts melted, they would never have doubted the existence of the Holy Ghost.

And now, beloved, it says, "He dwelleth with you, and shall be in you." We will close up with that sweet recollection—the Holy Ghost dwells in all believers and shall be with them.

One word of comment and advice to the saints of God, and to sinners, and I have done. Saints of the Lord! ye have this morning heard that God the Holy Ghost is a person; ye have had it proved to your souls. What follows from this? Why, it followeth how earnest ye should be in prayer to the Holy Spirit, as well as for the Holy Spirit. Let me say that this is an inference that you should lift up your prayers to the Holy Ghost: that you should cry earnestly unto him; for he is able to do exceeding abundantly above all you can speak or think. See this mass of people. What is to convert it? See this crowd? Who is to make my influence permeate through the mass? You know this place now has a mighty influence, and, God blessing us, it will have an influence not only upon this city, but upon England at large; for we now employ the press as well as the pulpit; and certainly, I should say, before the close of the year, more than two hundred thousand of my productions will be scattered through the land—words uttered by my lips, or written by my pen. But how can this influence be rendered for good? How shall God's glory be promoted by it? Only by incessant prayer for the Holy Spirit; by constantly calling down the influence of the Holy Ghost upon us; we want him to rest upon every page that is printed, and upon every word that is uttered. Let us then be doubly earnest in pleading with the Holy Ghost, that he would come and own our labors; that the whole church at large may be revived thereby, and not ourselves only, but the whole world share in the benefit.

Then, to the ungodly, I have this one closing word to say. Ever be careful how you speak of the Holy Ghost. I do not know what the unpardonable sin is, and I do not think any man understands it; but it is something like this: "He that speaketh a word against the Holy Ghost, it shall never be forgiven him." I do not know what that means; but tread carefully! There is danger; there is a pit which our ignorance has covered by sand; tread carefully! you may be in it before the next hour. If there is any strife in your heart to-day, perhaps you will go to the ale-house and forget it. Perhaps there is some voice speaking in your soul, and you will put it away. I do not tell you will be resisting the Holy Ghost, and committing the unpardonable sin; but it is somewhere there. Be very careful. O, there is no crime on earth so black as the crime against the Holy Spirit! Ye may blaspheme the Father, and ye shall be damned for it, unless ye repent; ye may blaspheme the Son, and hell shall be your portion, unless ye are forgiven; but blaspheme the Holy Ghost, and thus saith the Lord: "There is no forgiveness, either in this world nor in the world which is to come." I cannot tell you what it is; I do no profess to understand it; but there it is. It is the danger signal; stop! man, stop! If thou has despised the Holy Spirit— if thou hast laughed at his revelations, and scorned what Christians call his influence, I beseech thee, stop! This morning seriously deliberate. Perhaps some of you have actually committed the unpardonable sin; stop! Let fear stop you; sit down. Do not drive on so rashly as you have done, Jehu! O slacken your reins! Thou who are such a profligate in sin—thou who hast uttered such hard words against the Trinity, stop! Ah! it makes us all stop. It makes us all draw up, and say, "Have I not perhaps so done?" Let us think of this; and let us not at any time stifle either with the words or the acts of God the Holy Ghost.

Chapter 2
THE HOLY SPIRIT'S CHIEF OFFICE

"He shall glorify me: for he shall receive of mine, and shall shew it unto you. All things that the Father hath are mine: therefore said I, that he shall take of mine, and shall show it unto you"—John 16:14-15.

It is the chief office of the Holy Spirit to glorify Christ. He does many things, but this is what he aims at in all of them, to glorify Christ. Brethren, what the Holy Ghost does must be right for us to imitate: therefore, let us endeavour to glorify Christ. To what higher ends can we "devote ourselves, than to something to which God the Holy Ghost devotes himself? Be this, then, your emotional prayer, "Blessed Spirit, help me ever to glorify the Lord Jesus Christ!"

Observe, that the Holy Ghost glorifies Christ by showing to us the things of Christ. It is a great marvel that there should be any glory given to Christ by showing him to such poor creatures as we are. What! To make us see Christ, does that glorify him? For our weak eyes to behold him, for our trembling hearts to know him, and to love him, does this glorify him? It is even so, for the Holy Ghost chooses this as his principal way of glorifying the Lord Jesus. He takes of the things of Christ, not to show them to angels, not to write them in letters of fire across the brow of night, but to show them unto us. Within the little temple of a sanctified heart, Christ is praised, not so much by what we do, or think, as by what we see. This puts great value upon meditation, upon the study of God's word, and upon silent thought under the teaching of the Holy Spirit, for Jesus says, "He shall glorify me: for he shall receive of mine, and shall shew it unto you."

Here is a gospel word at the very outset of our sermon. Poor sinner, conscious of your sin, it is possible for Christ to be glorified by him being shown unto you. If you look to him, if you see him to be a suitable Saviour, an all-sufficient Saviour, if your mind's eye takes him in, if he is effectually shown to you by the Holy Spirit, he is thereby glorified. Sinner as you are, unworthy apparently to become the arena of Christ's glory, yet shall you be a temple in which the King's glory shall be revealed, and you poor heart, like a mirror, shall reflect his grace.

"Come, Holy Spirit, heavenly Dove,

With all thy quickening powers;"

and show Christ to the sinner, that Christ may be glorified in the sinner's salvation!

If that great work of grace is really done at the beginning of the sermon, I shall not mind even if I never finish it. God the Holy Ghost will have wrought more without me than I could possibly have wrought myself, and to the Triune Jehovah shall be all the praise. Oh, that the name of Christ may be glorified in every one of you! Has the Holy Spirit shown you Christ, the Sin-bearer, the one sacrifice for sin, exalted on high, to give repentance and remission? If so, then the Holy Spirit has glorified Christ, even in you.

Now proceeding to examine the text a little in detail, my first observation upon it is this, the Holy Spirit is our Lord's Glorifier: "He shall glorify me." Secondly, Christ's own things are his best glory: "He shall glorify me: for he shall shew it unto you;" and, thirdly, Christ's glory is his Father's glory: "all things that the Father hath are mine: therefore said I, that he shall take of mine, and shall shew it unto you."

I. To begin, then, the HOLY SPIRIT IS OUR LORD'S GLORIFIER. I want you to keep this truth in your mind, and never to forget it; that which does not glorify Christ is not of the Holy Spirit, and that which is of the Holy Spirit invariably glorifies our Lord Jesus Christ.

First, then, have an eye to this truth in all comforts. If a comfort which you think you need, and which appears to you to be very sweet, does not glorify Christ, look very suspiciously upon it. If, in conversing with an apparently religious man, he prates about truth which he says is comforting, but which does not honour Christ, do not you have anything to do with it. It is a poisonous sweet; it may charm you for a moment, but it will ruin your soul for ever if you partake of it. But blessed are those comforts which smell of Christ, those consolations in which there is a fragrance of myrrh, and aloes, and cassia, out of the King's palace, the comfort drawn from his person, from his work, from his blood, from his resurrection, from his glory, the comfort directly fetched from that sacred spot where he trod the wine-press alone. This is wine of which you may drink, and forget your misery, and be unhappy no more; but always look with great suspicion upon any comfort offered to you, either as a sinner or a saint, which does not come distinctly from Christ. Say, "I will not be comforted till Jesus comforts me. I will refuse to lay aside my despondency until he removes my sin. I will not go to Mr. Civility, or Mr. Legality, for the unloading of my burden; no hands shall ever life the load of conscious sin from off my heart but those that were nailed to the cross, when Jesus himself bore my sins in his own body on the tree." Please carry this truth with you wherever you go, as a kind of spiritual litmus paper, by which you may test everything that is presented to you as a cordial or comfort. If it does not glorify Christ, let it not console or please you.

In the next place, have an eye to this truth in all ministries. There are many ministries in the world, and they are very diverse from one another; but this truth will enable you to judge which is right out of them all. That ministry which makes much of Christ, is of the Holy Spirit; and that ministry which decries him, ignores him, or puts him in the background in any degree, is not of the Spirit of God. Any doctrine which magnifies man, but not man's Redeemer, any doctrine which denies the depth of the Fall, and consequently derogates from the greatness of salvation, any doctrine which makes sinless, and therefore makes Christ's work less,—away with it, away with it. This shall be you infallible test as to whether it is of the Holy Ghost or not, for Jesus says, "He shall glorify me." IT WERE BETTER TO SPEAK FIVE WORDS TO the GLORY OF CHRIST, THAN TO BE the greatest orator who ever lived, and to neglect or dishonour the Lord Jesus Christ. We, my brethren, who are preachers of the Word, have but a short time to live; let us dedicate all that time to the glorious work of magnifying Christ. Longfellow says, in his Psalm of Life, that "Art is long," but longer still is the great art of lifting up the Crucified before the eyes of the sin-bitten sons of men. Let us keep to that one employment. If we have but this one string upon which we can play, we may discourse such music on it as would ravish angels, and will save men; therefore, again I say, let us keep to that alone. Coronet, flute, harp, sackbut, psaltery, dulcimer, and all kinds of music are for Nebuchadnezzar's golden image; but as for our God, our one harp is Christ Jesus. We will touch every string of that wondrous instrument, even though it be with trembling fingers, and marvellous shall be the music we shall evoke from it.

All ministries, therefore, must be subjected to this test; if they do not glorify Christ, they are not of the Holy Ghost.

We should also have an eye to this truth in all religious movements, and judge them by this standard. If they are of the Holy Spirit, they glorify Christ. There are great movements in the world every now and then; we are inclined to look upon them hopefully, for any stir is better than stagnation; but, by-and-by we begin to fear, with a holy jealousy, what their effects will be. How shall we judge them? To what test shall we put them? Always to this test. Does this movement glorify Christ? Is Christ preached? Then therein I do rejoice, yea, and will rejoice. Are men pointed to Christ? Then this is the ministry of salvation. Is he preached as first and last? Are men bidden to be justified by faith in him, and then to follow him, and copy his divine example? It is well. I do not believe that any man ever lifted up the cross of Christ in a hurtful way. If it be but the cross that is seen, it is the sight of the cross, not of the hands that lift it, that will bring salvation. Some modern movements are heralded with great noise, and some come quietly; but if they glorify Christ, it is well. But dear friends, if it is some new theory that is propounded, if it is some old error revived, if it is something very glittering and fascinating, and for a while it bears the multitudes away, think nothing of it; unless it glorifies Christ it is not for you and me. "Aliquid Christi," as one of the old fathers said, "Anything of Christ," and I love it; but nothing of Christ, or something against Christ, then it may be very fine and flowery, and it may be very fascinating and charming, highly poetical, and in consonance with the spirit of the age; but we say of it, "Vanity of vanities, all is vanity where there is no Christ." Where he is uplifted, there is all that is wanted for the salvation of a guilty race. Judge every movement, then, not by those who adhere to it, nor by those who admire and praise it, but by this word of our Lord, "He shall glorify me." The Spirit of God is not in it if it does not glorify Christ.

Once again, brethren, I pray you, eye this truth when you are under a sense of great weakness, physical, mental, or spiritual. You have finished preaching a sermon, you have completed a round with your tracts, or you have ended your Sunday-School work for another Sabbath. You say to yourself, "I fear that I have done very poorly." You groan as you go to your bed because you think that you have not glorified Christ. It is as well that you should groan if that is the case. I will not forbid it, but I will relieve the bitterness of your distress by reminding you that it is the Holy Ghost who is to glorify Christ: "He shall glorify me." If I preach, and the Holy Spirit is with me, Christ will be glorified; but if I were able to speak with the tongues of men, and of angels, but without the power of the Holy Ghost, Christ would not be glorified. Sometimes, our weakness may even help to make way for the greater display of the might of God. If so, we may glory in infirmity, that the power of Christ may rest upon us. It is not merely we who speak, but the Spirit of the Lord, who speaketh by us. There is a sound of abundance of rain outside the Tabernacle; would God that there were also the sound of abundance of rain within our hearts! May the Holy Spirit come at this moment, and come at all times whenever his servants are trying to glorify Christ, and himself do what must always be his own work! How can you and I glorify anybody, much less glorify him who is infinetly glorious? But the Holy Ghost, being himself the glorious God, can glorify the glorious Christ. It is a work worthy of God; and it shows us, when we think of it, the absolute need of our crying to the Holy Spirit that he would take us in his hand, and use us as a workman uses his hammer. What can a hammer do without the hand that grasps it, and what can we do without the Spirit of God?

I will make only one more observation upon this first point. If the Holy Spirit is to glorify Christ, I beg you to have an eye to this truth amid all oppositions, controversies, and contentions. If we alone had the task of glorifying Christ, we might be beaten; but as the Holy Spirit is the Glorifier of Christ, his glory is in very safe hands. "Why do the heathen rage, and the people imagine a vain thing?" The Holy Spirit is still to the front; the eternal purpose of God to set his King upon the throne, and to make Jesus Christ reign for ever and ever, must be fulfilled, for the Holy Ghost has undertaken to see it accomplished. Amidst the surging tumults of the battle, the result of the conflict is never in doubt for a moment. It may seem as though the fate of Christ's cause hung in a balance, and that the scales were in equilibrium; but it is not so. The glory of Christ never wanes; it must increase from day to day, as it is made known in the hearts of men by the Holy Spirit; and the day shall come when Christ's praise shall go up from all human tongues. To him every knee shall bow, and every tongue shall confess that Jesus Christ is Lord, to the glory of God the Father. Therefore, lift up the hands that hang down, and confirm the feeble knees. If you have failed to glorify Christ by your speech as you would, there is Another who has done it, and who will still do it, according to Christ's words, "He shall glorify me." My text seems to be a silver bell, ringing sweet comfort into the dispirited worker's ear. "He shall glorify me."

That is the first point, the Holy Spirit is our Lord's Glorifier. Keep that truth before your mind's eye under all circumstances.

II. Now, secondly, CHRIST'S OWN THINGS ARE HIS BEST GLORY. When the Holy Spirit wants to glorify Christ, what does he do? He does not go abroad for anything, he comes to Christ himself for that which will be for Christ's own glory: "He shall glorify me: for he shall receive of mine, and shall shew it unto you." There can be no glory added to Christ; it must be his own glory, which he has already, which is made more apparent to the hearts of God's chosen by the Holy Spirit.

First of all, Christ needs no new inventions to glorify him. "We have struck out a new line of things," says one. Have you? "We have found out something very wonderful." I dare say you have; but Christ, the same yesterday, to-day, and for ever, wants none of your inventions, or discoveries, or additions to his truth. A plain Christ is ever the loveliest Christ. Dress him up, and you have deformed him and defamed him. Bring him out just as he is, the Christ of God, nothing else but Christ, unless you bring in his cross, for we preach Christ crucified; indeed, you cannot have the Christ without the cross; but preach Christ crucified, and you have given him all the glory that he wants. The Holy Ghost does not reveal in these last times any fresh ordinances, or any novel doctrines, or any new evolutions; but he simply brings to mind the things which Christ himself spoke, he brings Christ's own things to us, and in that way glorifies him.

Think for a minute of Christ's person as revealed to us by the Holy Spirit. What can more glorify him than for us to see his person, very God of very God, and yet as truly man? What a wondrous being, as human as ourselves, but as divine as God! Was there ever another like to him? Never.

Think of his incarnation, his birth at Bethlehem. There was greater glory among the oxen in the stall than ever was seen where those born in marble halls were swathed in purple and fine linen. Was there ever another babe like Christ? Never. I wonder not that the wise men fell down to worship him.

Look at his life, the standing wonder of all ages. Men, who have not worshipped him, have admired him. His life is incomparable, unique; there is nothing like it in all the history of mankind. Imagination has never been able to invent anything approximating to the perfect beauty of the life of Jesus Christ.

Think of his death. There have been may heroic and martyr deaths; but there is not one that can be set side by side with Christ's death. He did not pay the debt of natures as others do; and yet he paid our nature's debt. He did not die because he must; he died because he would. The only "must" that came upon him was a necessity of all-conquering love. The cross of Christ is the greatest wonder of fact or of fiction; fiction invents many marvellous things, but nothing than can be looked at for a moment in comparison with the cross of Christ.

Think of our Lord's resurrection. If this be one of the things that are taken, and shown to you by the Holy Spirit, it will fill you with holy delight. I am sure that I could go into that sepulchre, where John and Peter went, and spend a lifetime in revencing him who broke down that barriers of the tomb, and made it a passage-way to heaven. Instead of being a dungeon and a cul-de-sac, into which all men seem to go, but could ever come out, Christ has, by his resurrection, made a tunnel right through the grave. Jesus, by dying, has killed death for all believers.

Then think of his ascension. But why need I take you over all these scenes with which you are blessedly familiar? What a wondrous fact that, when the cloud received him out of the disciple's sight, the angels came to convoy him to his heavenly home!

"They brought his chariot from above,
To bear him to his throne;
Clapp'd their triumphant wings, and cried,
'The glorious work is done.'"

Think of him now, at his Father's right hand, adored of all the heavenly host; and then let your mind fly forward to the glory of his Second Advent, the final judgment with its terrible terrors, the millennium with its indescribable bliss, and the heaven of heavens, with its endless and unparalled splendour. If these things are shown to you by the Holy Spirit, the beatific vision will indeed glorify Christ, and you will sit down, and sing with the blessed Virgin, "My soul doth magnify the Lord, and my spirit hath rejoiced in God my Saviour."

Thus, you see that the things which glorify Christ are all in Christ; the Holy Spirit fetches nothing from abroad, but he takes of the things of Christ; and shows them unto us. The glory of kings lies in their silver and their gold, their silk and their gems; but the glory of Christ lies in himself. If we want to glorify a man, we bring him presents; if we wish to glorify Christ; we must accept presents from him. Thus we take the cup of salvation, calling upon the name of the Lord, and in so doing we glorify Christ.

Notice, next that these things of Christ's are too bright for us to see till the

Spirit shows them to us. We cannot see them because of their excessive glory, until the Holy Spirt, tenderly reveals them to us, until he takes of the things of Christ, and shows them to us.

What does this mean? Does it not mean, first, that he enlightens our understandings? It is wonderful how the Holy Spirit can take a fool, and make him know the wonders of Christ's dying love; and he does make him know it very quickly when he begins to teach him. Some of us have been very slow learners, yet the Holy Spirit has been able to teach something even to us. He opens the Scriptures, and he also opens our minds; and when there are these two openings together, what a wonderful opening it is! It becomes like a new revelation; the first is the revelation of the letter, which we have in the Book; the second is the revelation of the Spirit, which we get in our own spirit. O my dear friend, if the Holy Ghost has ever enlightened your understanding, you know what it is for him to show the things of Christ to you!

But next, he does this by a work upon the whole soul. I mean this. When the Holy Ghost convinces us of sin, we become fitted to see Christ, and so the blessed Spirit shows Christ to us. When we are conscious of our feebleness, then we see Christ's strength; and thus the Holy Ghost shows him to us. Often, the operations of the Spirit of God may seem not to be directly the showing of Christ to us, but as they prepare us for seeing him, they are a part of the work.

The Holy Ghost sometimes shows Christ to us by his power of vivifying the truth. I do not know whether I can quite tell you what I mean; but I have sometimes seen a truth differently from what I have ever seen it before. I knew it long ago, I owned it as part of the divine revelation; but now I realize it, grip it, grasp it, or what is better, it seems to get a grip of me, and hold me in its mighty hands. Have you not sometimes been overjoyed with a promise which never seemed anything to you before? Or a doctrine, which you believed, but never fully appreciated, has suddenly become to you a gem of the first water, a very Koh-I-Noor, or, "Mountain of Light." The Holy Spirit has a way of focussing light, and when it falls in this special way upon a certain point, then the truth is revealed to us. He shall take of the things of Christ, and show them unto you. Have you never felt ready to jump for joy, ready to start from your seat, ready to sit up in your bed at night, and sing praises to God through the overpowering influence of some grand old truth which has seemed to be all at once quite new to you?

The Holy Spirit also shows to us the things of Christ in our experience. As we journey on in life, we pass up hill and down dale, through bright sunlight and through dark shadows, and in each of these conditions we learn a little more of Christ, a little more of his grace, a little more of his glory, a little more of his sin-bearing, a little more of his glorious righteousness. Blessed is the life which is just one long lesson upon the glory of Christ; and I think that is what every Christian life should be. "Every dark and bending line" in our experience should meet in the centre of Christ's glory, and should lead us nearer and nearer to the power of enjoying the bliss at his right hand for ever and ever. Thus the Holy Spirit takes of the things of Christ, and shows them to us, and so glorifies Christ.

Beloved, the practical lesson for us to learn is this, let us try to abide under the influence of the Holy Spirit. To than end, let us think very reverently of him. Some never think of him at all. How many sermons there are without even an allusion to him! Shame on the preachers of such discourses! If any hearers come without praying for the Holy Spirit, shame on such hearers! We know and we confess that he is everything to our spiritual life; then why do we not remember him with greater love, and worship him with greater honour, and think of him continually with greater reverence? Beware of committing the sin against the Holy Ghost. If any of you feel any gentle touches of his power when you are hearing a sermon, beware lest you harden your heart against it. Whenever the sacred fire comes as but a spark, quench not the Holy Spirit, but pray that the spark may become a flame. And you, Christian people, do cry to him that you may not read your Bibles without his light. Do not pray without being helped by the Spirit; above all, may you never preach without the Holy Spirit! It seems a pity when a man asks to be guided of the Spirit in his preaching, and then pulls out a manuscript, and reads it. The Holy Sprit may bless what he reads; but he cannot very well guide him when he has tied himself down to what he has written. And it will be the same with the speaker if he only repeats what he has learnt, and leaves no room for the Spirit to give him a new thought, a fresh revelation of Christ; how can he hope for the divine blessing under such circumstances? Oh, it were better for us to sit still until some of us were moved by the Spirit to get up and speak, than for us to prescribe the methods by which he should speak to us, and even to write down the very words we mean to utter! What room is there for the Spirit's operations then?

"Come Holy Spirit, heavenly Dove,"

I cannot help breaking out into that prayer, "Blessed Spirit, abide with us, take of the things of Christ, and show them to us, that so Christ may be glorified."

III. I am only going to speak a minute or two on the last point. It is a very deep one, much too deep for me. I am unable to take you into the depths of my text, I will not pretend to do so; I believe that there are meanings here which probably we shall never understand till we get to heaven. "What thou knowest not now, thou shalt know hereafter." But this is the point, CHRIST'S GLORY IS HIS FAtheR'S GLORY: "All things that the Father hath are mine: therefore I said I, that he shall take of mine, and shall shew it unto you."

First, Christ has all that the Father has. Do think that. No more man dares to say, "All things that the Father hath are mine." All the Godhead is in Christ; not only all the attributes of it, but the essence of it. The Nicene Creed well puts it, and it is not too strong in the expression: "Light of Light, very God of very God," for Christ has all that the Father has. When we come to Christ, we come to omnipotent omnipresent omniscience; we come to almighty immutability; we come, in fact, to the eternal Godhead. The Father has all things, and all power is given unto Christ in heaven and on earth, so that he has all that the Father has.

And further, the Father is glorified in Christ's glory. Never let us fall into the false notion that, if we magnify Christ, we are depreciating the Father. If any lips have ever spoken concerning the Christ of God so as to depreciate the God of Christ, let those lips be covered with shame. We never did preach Christ up as merciful, and the Father as only just, or Christ as moving the Father to be gracious. That is a slander which has been cast upon us, but there is not an atom of truth in it. We have known and believed what Christ himself said, "I and My Father are one." The more glorious Christ is, the more glorious the Father is; and when men, professedly Christians, begin to cast off Christ, they cast off God the Father to a large extent. Irreverence to the Son of God soon becomes irreverence to God the Father himself. But dear friends, we delight to honour Christ, and we will continue to do so. Even when we stand in the heaven of heavens, before the burning throne of the infinite Jehovah, we will sing praises unto him and unto the Lamb, putting the two evermore in that divine conjunction in which they are always to be found.

Thus, you see, Christ has all that the Father has, and when he is glorified, the Father also is glorified.

Next, the Holy Spirit must lead us to see this, and I am sure that he will. If we give ourselves up to his teaching, we shall fall into no errors. It will be a great mystery, but we shall know enough, so that it will never trouble us. If you sit down and try to study the mystery of the Eternal, well, I believe that the longer you look, the more you will be like persons who look into the sea from a great height, until they grow dizzy, and are ready to fall and to be drowned. Believe what the Spirit teaches you, and adore your Divine Teacher; then shall his instruction become easy to you. I believe that, as we grow older, we come to worship God as Abraham did, as Jehovah, the great I AM. Jesus does not fade into the background; but the glorious Godhead seems to become more and more apparent to us. Our Lord's word to his disciples, "Ye believe in God, believe also in me." And as we come to full confidence in the glorious Lord, the God of nature, and of providence, and of redemption, and of heaven, the Holy Spirit gives us to know more of the glories of Christ.

I have talked with you as well as I could upon this sublime theme, and if I did not know that the Holy Spirit glorifies Christ, I should go home miserable, for I have not been able to glorify my Lord as I would; but I know that the Holy Spirit can take what I have said out of my very heart, and can put it into your hearts, and he can add to it whatever I have omitted. Go ye who love the Lord, and glorify him. Try to do it by your lips and by your lives. Go ye, and preach him, preach more of him, and preach him up higher and higher, and higher. The old lady, of whom I have heard, made a mistake in what she said, yet there was a truth behind her blunder. She had been to a little Baptist chapel, where a high Calvinist preached, and on coming away she said that she liked "High Calvary" preachers best. So do I. Give me a "High Calvary" preacher, one who will make Calvary the highest of all the mountains. I suppose it was not a hill at all, but only a mound; still, let us lift it higher and higher, and say to all other hills, "Why leap ye, ye high hills? This is the hill which God desires to dwell in; year, the Lord will dwell in it forever." The crucified Christ is wiser than all the wisdom of the world. The cross of Christ has more novelty in it than all the fresh things of the earth. O believers and preachers of the gospel, glorify Christ! May the Holy Ghost help you to do so!

And you, poor sinners, who think that you cannot glorify Christ at all, come and trust him,—"Come naked, come filthy, come just as you are," and believe that he will receive you; for that will glorify him. Believe, even now, O sinner at death's door, that Christ can make thee live; for thy faith will glorify him! Look up out of the awful depths of hell into which conscience has cast thee, and believe that he can pluck thee out of the horrible pit, and out of the miry clay, and set thy feet upon a rock; for thy trust will glorify him! It is in the power of the sinner to give Christ the greatest glory, if the Holy Spirit enables him to believe in the Lord Jesus Christ. Thou mayest come, thou who art more leprous, more diseased, more corrupt, than any other; and if thou lookest to him, and he saves thee, oh, then thou wilt praise him! You will be of the mind of the one I have spoken of many times, who said to me, "Sir, you say that Christ can save me. Well, if he does, he shall never hear the last of it." No, and he never will hear the last of it. Blessed Jesus,—

"I will love thee in life, I will love thee in death,
And praise thee as long as thou lendest me breath;
And say when the death-dew lies cold on my brow,
If ever I loved thee, my Jesus, 'Tis now.
"In mansion of glory and endless delight,
I'll ever adore thee in heaven so bright;
I'll sing with the glittering crown on my brow,
If ever I loved thee, my Jesus, 'tis now."

We will do nothing else but praise Christ, and glorify him, if he will but save us from sin. God grant that it may be so with every one of us, for the Lord Jesus Christ's sake! Amen.

JOHN 16:1-16. EXPOSITION by C. H. Spurgeon

Verse 1. *These things have I spoken unto you, that ye should not be offended.*

Or, "made to stumble." Christ would not have you who are his people caused to stumble by anything that happens to you. He wants you to walk without tripping; his angels bear you up in their hands lest at any time you should dash your foot against a stone. He himself, as your Guardian, comes and speaks before hand to let you know what is to occur to you, that you may not be caused to stumble by any fresh trial that may assail you.

2. *They shall put you out of the synagogues: yea, the time cometh, that whosoever killeth you will think that he doeth God service.*

Christ's disciples were to expect opposition of the most cruel kind. They were to be put away from those with whom they had long worshipped; they were even to run the risk of losing their lives; but Jesus foretold what would happen to them, that they might not be stumbled at it. Such was their Lord's love to them that he would not have them attacked unawares; by his grace, they would hold on, and hold out, they would persevere to the end; but there would have to be a struggle, and to help them in the fight, Jesus tells them all about it before it begins. We say, "Forewarned, forearmed." So the disciples were; and so are you. Your Lord tells you that you will not get to heaven without trials: "In the world ye shall have tribulation." And he tells you this that it may not surprise you when it comes, that it may not act upon you like a sudden gust of wind that would upset a little ship; but that you may just keep everything in trim looking for the storm to come: "These things have I spoken unto you, that ye should not be caused to stumble."

3. And these things will they do unto you, because they have not known the Father, nor me.

The persecuting Jews professed to be worshippers of Jehovah; but they did not know the Christ, whom he sent, and, therefore, in very truth they did not know the Father either. How can you expect that those who do not know the Father will know the Son, or any of the other children of the divine family? As they rejected the Elder Brother, will they not also reject the younger ones? Is the disciple to be above his Master, or the servant to be treated better than his Lord? Think not so; and therefore expect that you will not be known, even as the Father and the Son were not known.

"'Tis no surprising thing,
That we should be unknown:
The Jewish world knew not their King,
God's everlasting Son."

4. But these things have I told you, that when the time shall come, ye may remember that I told you of them. And these things I said not unto you at the beginning, because I was with you.

Our Lord did tell his disciples something about "these things." He did warn them to expect opposition, but he did not dwell upon that theme, he did not expatiate upon it. He did not at first give that prominence to it which he was about to do, and he explains to his disciples why he had not talked much upon that topic: "because I was with you." It did not matter how they were opposed so long as he was with them; his society more than made up for anything they might have to suffer; and, dear child or God, if you now enjoy the presence of Christ, and the power of his Spirit, you need not mind what happens to you.

5, 6. But now I go my way to him that sent me; and none of you asketh me, Whither goest thou? But because I have said these things unto you, sorrow hath filled your heart.

They were cast down because he was going away from them. Love awoke fear. It was a hard thing for them to have to miss him; they could not tell what might happen to them when their Leader was gone from their midst. Do you wonder that they were filled with sorrow? Yet there was no real cause for grief; there was rather reason for rejoicing when they understood the true lesson of Christ's departure. There is no real cause for your sorrow, dear friends. If you know all things, you would rejoice exceedingly in that very thing that now most troubles you.

7. Nevertheless I tell you the truth; It is expedient for you that I go away: for if I go not away, the Comforter will not come unto you; but if I depart, I will send him unto you.

And the Comforter is better for us that the personal presence of Christ. We do not always think so; but it is true. It is better for the Church to have the Holy Spirit in the midst of her, than for Christ to be here in the bodily presence on the earth.

8. And when he is come, he will reprove the world of sin, and of righteousness, and of judgment:

The world is not as yet convinced, but it is convicted; though it does not own its guilt, there is more than sufficient evidence to prove it guilty in the sight of God.

9. Of Sin, because they believe not on me;

What must be the depth of human wickedness that sinners will not accept a Divine Saviour! This is the crowning, crushing proof of human guilt: "They believe not on me."

10. Of righteousness, because I go to my Father, and ye see me no more;

Christ was righteous, the righteous One, whom men rejected, for he has gone up to the Father's side, where he could not have been if he had not perfected righteousness. The very going back of Christ to the Father's throne proves that righteousness does exist, and convicts men of sinning against it.

11. Of judgment, because the prince of this world is judged.

The gospel judges him, and dethrones him; and as there has been a judgment of the world's king, so there will be a judgment of the world itself.

12. I have yet many things to say unto you, but ye cannot bear them now.

Some teachers overload their hearers with truth till I might truly say that they pile on the agony. Truth which cannot be received is often most irksome and burdensome to the hearer; when the mind is not in a fit condition to bear any more instruction, it is cruel work to impose it. Our Lord Jesus did not so overburden his disciples: "I have yet many things to say unto you, but ye cannot bear them now."

13. Howbeit when he, the Spirit of truth, is come, he will guide you into all truth: for he shall not speak of himself;

This is a very wonderful expression: "He shall not speak of himself." We have plenty of men, nowadays, who boast that they do speak of or from themselves; that is to say, they profess to borrow from no one, not even from God. They are original thinkers, inventors; they bring forth fresh things out of the depth of their wonderful minds; but even the Holy Ghost is here said not to "speak of himself."

13. But whatsoever he shall hear, that shall he speak;

That is just our business, to hear God's message, and then to speak it; and if the Holy Ghost does this, and if Jesus did it, we also may be glad to do the same. We are no inventors of great novelties; we are simply the message-bearers of the Most High, the declarers of the old truths which God has revealed to us.

13-16. And he will shew you things to come. He shall glorify me: for he shall receive of mine, and shall shew it unto you. All things that the Father hath are mine: therefore said I, that he shall take of mine, and shall shew it unto you. A little while, and ye shall not see me: and again, a little while, and ye shall see me, because I go to the Father.

How wonderful this is! We are to see Jesus because he has gone to the Father. It looks as if that were a reason why we should not see him; but we see him better, by faith, now that he has gone to the Father, than we could have seen him while he was here below covered with the veil of his humiliation. Yet it is hardly surprising that the disciples were puzzled by their Lord's words: "A little while, and ye shall not see me: and again, a little while, and ye shall see me:" and, "Because I go to the Father."

Chapter 3
THE HOLY SPIRIT GLORIFYING CHRIST

"He will glorify Me: for He shall receive of Mine, and shall show it unto you."—John 16:14.

    The needs of spiritual men are very great, but they cannot be greater than the power of the Divine Trinity is able to meet. We have one God-Father, Son, and Holy Spirit-One in Three, and Three in One; and that blessed Trinity in Unity gives Himself to sinners that they may be saved. In the first place, every good thing that a sinner wants is in the Father. The prodigal son was wise when he said, "I will arise and go to my father." Every good and perfect gift comes from God the Father, the first Person in the blessed Trinity, because every good gift and every perfect gift can only be found in Him. But the needy soul says, "How shall I get to the Father? He is infinitely above me. How shall I reach up to Him?" In order that you might obtain the blessings of grace, God was in Christ Jesus, the second ever-blessed Person of the Sacred Trinity. Let me read you part of the verse that follows my text: "All things that the Father has are Mine." So you see, everything is in the Father first; and the Father puts all things into Christ. "It pleased the Father that in Him should all fullness dwell." Now you can get to Christ because He is man as well as God. He is "over all, God blessed forever;" but He came into this world, was born of the Virgin Mary, lived a life of poverty, "suffered under Pontius Pilate, was crucified, dead, and buried." He is the conduit conveying to us all blessings from the Father. In the Gospel of John we read, "Of His fullness have all we received, and grace for grace." Thus you see the Father, with every good thing in Himself, putting all fullness into the Mediator, the Man Christ Jesus who is also the Son of God.

    Now I hear a poor soul say, "But I cannot get to Christ; I am blind and lame. If I could get to Him, He would open my eyes; but I am so lame that I cannot run or even walk to Him. If I could get to Him, He would give me strength; but I lie as one dead. I cannot see Christ or tell where to find Him." Here comes in the work of the Holy Spirit, the third Person of the blessed

Unity. It is His office to take of the things of Christ, and show them unto saints and sinners, too. We cannot see them, but we shall see them fast enough when He shows them to us. Our sin puts a veil between us and Christ. The Holy Spirit comes and takes the veil away from our heart, and then we see Christ. It is the Holy Spirit's office to come between us and Christ, to lead us to Christ, even as the Son of God comes between us and the Father, to lead us to the Father; so that we have the whole Trinity uniting to save a sinner, the Triune God bowing down out of heaven for the salvation of rebellious men. Every time we dismiss you from this house of prayer, we pronounce upon you the blessing of the Sacred Trinity: "May the grace of our Lord Jesus Christ, and the love of God, and the communion of the Holy Spirit be with you!" And you need all that to make a sinner into a saint, and to keep a saint from going back to being a sinner again. The whole blessed Godhead, Father, Son, and Holy Spirit, must work upon every soul that is to be saved.

See how divinely they work together-how the Father glorifies the Son, how the Holy Spirit glorifies Jesus, how both the Holy Spirit and the Lord Jesus glorify the Father! These Three are One, sweetly uniting in the salvation of the chosen seed.

Tonight our work is to speak of the Holy Spirit. Oh, what a blessed Person He is; not merely a sacred influence, but a Divine Person, "very God of very God." He is the Spirit of holiness to be reverenced, to be spoken of with delight, yet with trembling; for, remember, there is a sin against the Holy Spirit. A word spoken against the Son of man may be forgiven, but blasphemy against the Holy Spirit (whatever that may be, I know not), is put down as a sin beyond the line of divine forgiveness. Therefore reverence, honor, and worship God the Holy Spirit, in whom lies the only hope that any of us can ever have of seeing Jesus, and so of seeing God the Father.

First, tonight, I shall try to speak of what the Holy Spirit does: "He shall receive of Mine, and shall show it unto you;" secondly, I shall seek to set forth what the Holy Spirit aims at: "He shall glorify Me: for He shall receive of Mine, and shall show it unto you;" and, thirdly, I shall explain how in both these things He acts as the Comforter, for we read, in the seventh verse, our Savior say, "If I go not away, the Comforter will not come unto you;" and it is of the Comforter that He says, "He shall glorify Me; for He shall receive of Mine, and shall show it unto you."

I. First, we are to consider WHAT THE HOLY SPIRIT DOES. Jesus says,

"He shall receive of Mine, and shall show it unto you."

The Holy Spirit, then, deals with the things of Christ. How I wish that all Christ's ministers would imitate the Holy Spirit in this respect! When you are dealing with the things of Christ, you are on Holy Spirit ground; you are following the track of the Holy Spirit. Does the Holy Spirit deal with science? What is science? Another name for the ignorance of men. Does the Holy Spirit deal with politics? What are politics? Another name for every man getting as much as he can out of the nation. Does the Holy Spirit deal with these things? No, my brethren, "He will receive of Mine." O my brother, the Holy Spirit will leave you if you go gadding about after these insignificant trifles! He will leave you, if you aim at magnifying yourself, and your wisdom, and your plans; for the Holy Spirit is taken up with the things of Christ. "He shall receive of Mine, and shall show it unto you." I like what Mr. Wesley said to his preachers. "Leave other things alone," said he; "you are called to win souls." So I believe it is with all true preachers. We may leave other things alone. The Holy Spirit, who is our Teacher, will own and bless us if we keep to His line of things. O preacher of the gospel, what can you receive like the things of Christ? And what can you talk of so precious to the souls of men as the things of Christ? Therefore, follow the Holy Spirit in dealing with the things of Christ.

Next, the Holy Spirit deals with feeble men. "He shall receive of Mine, and shall show it unto you." "Unto you." He is not above dealing with simple minds. He comes to those who have no training, no education, and He takes the things of Christ, and shows them to such minds. The greatest mind of man that was ever created was a poor puny thing compared with the infinite mind of God. We may boast about the great capacity of the human intellect; but what a narrow and contracted thing it is at its utmost width! So, for the Holy Spirit to come, and teach the little mind of man, is a great condescension. But we see the great condescension of the Holy Spirit even more when we read, "Not many wise men after the flesh, not many mighty, not many noble are called;" and when we hear the Savior say, "I thank You, O Father, Lord of heaven and earth, because You have hid these things from the wise and prudent, and have revealed them unto babes." The Holy Spirit takes of the things of Christ, and shows them to those who are babes compared with the wise men of this world. The Lord Jesus might have selected princes to be His apostles; He might have gathered together twelve of the greatest kings of the earth, or at least twelve senators from Rome; but he did not so. He took fishermen, and men belonging to that class, to be the pioneers of His kingdom; and God the Holy Spirit takes of the things of Christ, high and sublime as they are, and shows them unto men like these apostles were, men ready to follow where the Lord led them, and to learn what the Lord taught them.

If you think of the condescension of the Holy Spirit in taking of the things of Christ, and showing them to us, you will not talk any more about coming down to the level of children when you talk to them. I remember a young man who was a great fool, but did not know it, and therefore was all the greater fool; once, speaking to children, he said, "My dear children, it takes a great deal to bring a great mind down to your capacities." You cannot show me a word of Christ of that kind. Where does the Holy Spirit ever talk about its being a great come-down for Him to teach children, or to teach us? No, no; but He glorifies Christ by taking of His things, and showing them unto us, even such poor ignorant scholars as we are.

If I understand what is meant here, I think that it means, first, that the Holy Spirit helps us to under- stand the words of Christ. If we will study the teaching of the Savior, it must be with the Holy Spirit as the light to guide us; He will show us what Christ meant by the words He uttered. We shall not lose ourselves in the Savior's verbiage; but we shall get at the inner meaning of Christ's mind, and be instructed therein; for the Lord Jesus says, "He shall receive of Mine, and shall show it unto you." A sermon of Christ, even a single word of Christ, set in the light of the Holy Spirit, shines like a diamond; no, like a fixed star, with light that is never dim. Happy men and happy women who read the words of Christ in the light shed upon them by the Holy Spirit! But I do not think that this is all that the text means.

It means this: "Not only shall He reveal My words, but My things;" for Christ says, "All things that the Father has are Mine: therefore said I, that He shall take of Mine, and shall show it to you."

The Holy Spirit takes the nature of Christ, and shows it unto us. It is easy to say, "I believe Him to be God and man;" but the point is, to apprehend that He is God, and therefore able to save, and even to work impossibilities; and to believe that He is man, and therefore feels for you, sympathizes with you, and therefore is a brother born to help you in your adversities. May the Holy Spirit make you see the God- Man tonight! May He show you the humanity and the Deity of Christ, as they are most blessedly united in His adorable person; and you will be greatly comforted thereby.

The Holy Spirit shows to us the offices of Christ. He is Prophet, Priest, and King. Especially to you, sinner, Christ is a Savior. Now, if you know that He takes up the work of saving sinners, and that it is His business to save men, why then, dear friend, surely you will have confidence in Him, and not be afraid to come to Him! If I wanted my shoes mended, I would not take my hat off when I went into a cobbler's shop, and say, "Please excuse me. May I beg you to be so good as to mend my shoes?" No, it is his trade: it is his business. He is glad to see me. "What do you want, sir?" says he; and he is glad of work. And when Christ puts over His door, "Savior," I, needing to be saved, go to Him, for I believe that He knows His calling, and that He can carry it out, and that He will be glad to see me, and that I shall not be more glad to be saved than He will be to save me. I want you to catch that idea. If the Holy Spirit will show you that, it will bring you very near to joy and peace tonight.

May the Holy Spirit also show you Christ's engagements! He has come into the world engaged to save sinners. He pledged Himself to the Father to bring many sons unto glory, and He must do it. He has bound Himself to His Father, as the Surety of the covenant, that He will bring sinners into reconciliation with God. May the Holy Spirit show that fact to you; and right gladly you will leap into the Savior's arms!

It is very sweet when the Holy Spirit shows us the love of Christ-how intensely He loves men, how He loved them of old, for His delights were with the sons of men-not because He had redeemed them; but He redeemed them because He loved them, and delighted in them. Christ has had an eternal love to His people- "His heart is made of tenderness, His heart melts with love."

It is His heaven to bring men to heaven. It is His glory to bring sons to glory. He is never as happy as when He is receiving sinners. And if the Holy Spirit will show you the depth and the height, the length and the breadth of the love of Christ to sinners, it will go a long way towards bringing all who are in this house tonight to accept the Savior.

And when the Holy Spirit shows you the mercy of Christ-how willingly He forgives; how He passes by iniquity, transgression, and sin; how He casts your sins into the sea, throws them behind God's back, puts them away forever-ah! When you see this, then will your hearts be won to Him.

Especially I would desire the Holy Spirit to show you the blood of Christ. A Spirit-taught view of the blood of Christ is the most wonderful sight that ever a weeping eye beheld. There is your sin, your wicked, horrible, damnable sin; but Christ comes into the world, and takes the sin, and suffers in your room and place and stead; and the blood of such a One as He, perfect man and infinite God-such blood as was poured out on Calvary's tree-must take away sin. Oh, for a sight of it! If any of you are now despairing, and the Holy Spirit will take of the blood of Christ, and show it to you, despair will have no place in you any longer. It must be gone, for "the blood of Jesus Christ His Son cleanses us from all sin," and he that believes in Him is forgiven all his iniquities.

And if the Holy Spirit will also take of the prayers of Christ, and show them to you, what a sight you will have! Christ on earth, praying till He gets into a bloody sweat; Christ in heaven, praying with all His glorious vestments on, accepted by the Father, glorified at the Father's right hand, and making intercession for transgressors, praying for you, praying for all who come to God by Him, and able, therefore, to save them to the uttermost-this is the sight you will have! A knowledge of the intercession of Christ for guilty men is enough to make despair flee away once for all. I can only tell you these things; but if the Holy Spirit will take of them, and show them to you, oh, beloved, you will have joy and peace tonight through believing!

One thing I must add, however, and then I will leave this point, upon which we could dilate for six months, I think; that is, that whatever the Holy Spirit shows you, you may have. Do you see that? He takes of the things of Christ, and shows them to us; but why? Not as a boy at school does to one of his companions when he is teasing him. I remember often seeing it done. He pulls out of his pocket a beautiful apple, and shows it to his schoolmate. "There," he says, "do you see that apple?" Is he going to say, "Now I am going to give you a piece of it"? No, not he. He only shows him the apple to tantalize him. Now, it would be blasphemy to imagine that the Holy Spirit would show you the things of Christ, and then say, "You cannot have them." No, whatever He shows you, you may have. Whatever you see in Christ, you may have. Whatever the Holy Spirit makes you to see in the person and work of the Lord Jesus, you may have it. And He shows it to you on purpose that you may have it, for He is no Tantalus to mock us with the sight of a blessing beyond our reach; He waits to bless us. Lay that thought up in your heart; it may help you some day, if not now. You remember what God said to Jacob, "The land whereon you lie, to you will I give it." If you find any promise in this Book, and you dare to lie down upon it, it is yours. If you can just lie down and rest on it, it is yours; for it was not put there for you to rest on it without its being fulfilled to you. Only stretch yourself on any covenant blessing, and it is yours forever. God help us so to do!

II. But now, secondly, and very briefly, let us consider WHAT THE HOLY SPIRIT AIMS AT. Well, He aims at this, Jesus says, "He shall glorify Me." When He shows us the things of Christ, His objective is to glorify Christ. The Holy Spirit's objective is to make Christ appear to be great and glorious to you and to me. The Lord Jesus Christ is infinitely glorious; and even the Holy Spirit cannot make Him glorious except to our apprehension; but His desire is that we may see and know more of Christ, that we may honor Him more, and glorify Him more.

Well, how does the Holy Spirit go about this work? In this simple way, by showing us the things of Christ. Is not this a blessedly simple fact, that when even the Holy Spirit intends to glorify Christ, all that He does is to show us Christ? Well, but does He not put fine words together, and weave a spell of eloquence? No; He simply shows us Christ. Now, if you wanted to praise Jesus Christ tonight, what would you have to do? Why, you would only have to speak of Him as He is-holy, blessed, and glorious! You would show Him, as it were, in order to praise Him, for there is no glorifying Christ except by making Him to be seen. Then He has the glory that rightly belongs to Him. No words are wanted, no descriptions are needed. "He will glorify Me: for He shall receive of Mine, and shall show it unto you."

And is it not strange that Christ should be glorified by His being shown to you? To you, my dear friend! Perhaps you are saying, "I am a nobody." Yes, but Christ is glorified by being shown to you. "Oh, but I am very poor, very illiterate, and besides, very wicked!" Yes, but Christ is glorified by being shown to you. Now, a great king or a great queen would not be rendered much more illustrious by being shown to a little Sunday school girl, or exhibited to a crossing-sweeper boy. At least they would not think so; but Christ does not act as an earthly monarch might. He reckons it to be His glory for the poorest pair of eyes that ever wept to look by faith upon Him. He reckons it to be His greatest honor for the poorest man, the poorest woman, or the poorest child that ever lived, to see Him in the light in which the Holy Spirit sets Him. Is not this a blessed truth? I put it very simply and briefly. The Holy Spirit, you see, glorifies Christ by showing Him to sinners. Therefore, if you want to glorify Christ, do the same. Do not go and write a ponderous tome, and put fine words together. Tell sinners, in simple language, what Christ is. "I cannot praise Him," says one. You do not need to praise Him. Say what He is. If a man says to me, "Show me the sun," do I say, "Well, you must wait till I strike a match and light a candle, and then I will show you the sun"? That would be ridiculous, would it not? And for our candles to be held up to show Christ is absurd. Tell what He is. Tell what He is to you. Tell what He did for you. Tell what He did for sinners. That is all. "He shall glorify Me: for He shall receive of Mine, and shall show it unto you."

I will not say more on this point, except that, if any of us are to glorify Christ, we must talk much of Him. We must tell what the Holy Spirit has told to us; and we must pray the Holy Spirit to bless to the minds of men the truth we speak, by enabling them to see Christ as the Spirit reveals Him.

III. But now, thirdly, in both of these things-showing unto us the things of Christ, and glorifying Christ-THE HOLY SPIRIT IS A COMFORTER. Gracious Spirit, be a Comforter now to some poor struggling ones in the Tabernacle, by showing them the things of Christ, and by glorifying Him in their salvation!

First, in showing to men the things of Christ, the Holy Spirit is a Comforter. There is no comfort like a sight of Christ. Sinner, your only comfort must lie in your Savior, in His precious blood, and in His resurrection from the dead. Look that way, man! If you look inside, you will never find any comfort there. Look where the Holy Spirit looks. "He shall receive of Mine, and shall show it unto you." When a thing is shown to you, it is meant for you to look at it. If you want real comfort, I will tell you where to look, namely, to the person and work of the Lord Jesus Christ. "Oh!" you say, "but I am a wretched sinner." I know you are. You are a great deal worse than you think you are. "Oh, but I think myself the worst that ever lived." No, you are worse than that! You do not know half your depravity. You are worse than you ever dreamed you were. But that is not where to look for comfort. "I am brutish," says one; "I am proud; I am self-righteous; I am envious; I have everything in me that is bad, sir, and if I have a little bit that is good sometimes, it is gone before I can see it. I am just lost, ruined, and undone." That is quite true; but I never told you to look there. Your comfort lies in this, "He shall receive of Mine"-that is, of Christ's- "and shall show it unto you." Your hope of transformation, of gaining a new character altogether, of eternal life, lies in Christ, who, quickens the dead, and makes all things new. Look away from self, and look to Christ, for He alone can save you.

A sight of Christ is the destruction of despair. "Oh, but the devil tells me that I shall be cast into hell! There is no hope for me." What does it matter what the devil tells you? He was a liar from the beginning. Let him say what he likes; but if you will look away to Christ, that will be the end of the devil's power over you. If the Holy Spirit shows you what Christ came to do on the cross, and what He is doing on His throne in heaven, that will be the end of these troublous thoughts from Satan, and you will be comforted. Dear child of God, are you in sorrow tonight? May the Holy Spirit take of the things of Christ, and show them to you! There is an end to sorrow when you see Jesus, for sorrow itself is so sweetly sanctified by the companionship of Christ which it brings you, that you will be glad to drink of His cup and to be baptized with His baptism.

Are you in need tonight, without even a place where to lay your head? So, too, was He. "The Son of man has not where to lay His head." Go to Him with your trouble. He will help you to bear your poverty. He will help you to get out of it, for He is able to help you in temporal trials as well as in spiritual ones. Therefore go to Christ. All power is given unto Him in heaven and in earth. Nothing is too hard for the Lord. Go your way to Him, and a sight of Him will give you comfort.

Are you persecuted? Well, a sight of the thorn-crowned brow will take the thorn out of persecution. Are you very, very low? I think that you have all heard the story I am about to tell you, but some of you have, perhaps, forgotten it. Many years ago, when this great congregation first met in the Surrey Music Hall, and the terrible accident occurred, when many persons were either killed or wounded in the panic, I did my best to hold the people together till I heard that some were dead, and then I broke down like a man stunned, and for a fortnight or so I had little reason left. I felt so broken in heart that I thought that I would never be able to face a congregation again; and I went down to a friend's house, a few miles away, to be very quiet and still. I was walking round his garden, and I well remember the spot, and even the time, when this passage came to me, "Him has God exalted with His right hand to be a Prince and a Savior;" and this thought came into my mind at once, "You are only a soldier in the great King's army, and you may die in a ditch; but it does not matter what becomes of you as long as your King is exalted. He-HE is glorious. God has highly exalted Him." You have heard of the old French soldiers when they lay dying. If the emperor came by, when they were ready to expire, they would raise themselves up, and give one more cheer for their beloved leader. "Viva l'Empereur!" would be their dying words. And so I thought, "He is exalted. What matters it about me?" and in a moment my reason was perfectly restored. I was as clear as possible. I went into the house, had family prayer, and came back to preach to my congregation on the following Sabbath, restored only by having looked to Jesus, and having seen that He was glorious. If He is to the front, what does it matter what happens to us? Rank on rank we will die in the battle if He wins the victory. Only let the Man on the White Horse win; let the King who died for us, and washed us in His precious blood, be glorified, and it is enough for us.

But now, lastly, when Christ is glorified in the heart, He acts as a Comforter, too. I believe, brethren, that we would not have half the trouble that we have if we thought more of Christ. The fact is that we think so much of ourselves that we get troubled. But someone says, "But I have so many troubles." Why should you not have a great many troubles? Who are you that you should not have troubles? "Oh, but I have had loss after loss which you do not know of!" Very likely, dear friend, I do not know of your losses, but is it any wonder that you should have them? "Oh!" says one, "I seem to be kicked about like a football." Why should you not be? What are you? "Oh!" said one poor penitent to me the other night, "for me to come to Christ, sir, after my past life, seems so mean." I said, "Yes, so it is; but, then, you are mean. It was a mean business of the prodigal son to come home, and eat his father's bread and the fatted calf after he had spent his substance in riotous living." It was a mean thing, was it not? But then, the father did not think it mean. He clasped him to his bosom, and welcomed him home. Come along, you mean sinners, you that have served the devil, and now want to run away from him! Steal away from Satan at once, for my Lord is ready to receive you. You have no idea how willing He is to welcome you. He is so ready to forgive that you have not yet guessed how much sin He can forgive. "All manner of sin and blasphemy shall be forgiven unto men." Up to your necks in filth, in your very hearts saturated with the foulest iniquity; yet, if you come to Christ, He will wash you whiter than snow. "Come now, and let us reason together, says the Lord: though your sins be as scarlet, they shall be as white as snow; though they be red like crimson, they shall be as wool." Come along, and try my Lord.

Have exalted ideas of Christ. Oh, if a man will but have great thoughts of

Christ, he shall then find his troubles lessening, and his sins disappearing! You have been putting Christ on a wrong scale altogether, I see. Perhaps even you people of God have not thought of Christ as you ought to do. I have heard of a certain commander who had led his troops into a rather difficult position. He knew what he was doing, but the soldiers did not all know; and there would be a battle on the morrow. So he thought that he would go round from tent to tent, and hear what the soldiers said. He listened, and there was one of them saying to his fellows, "See what a mess we are in now! Do you see, we have only so many cavalry, and so many infantry, and we have only a small quantity of artillery. And on the other side there are so many thousands against us, so strong, so mighty, that we shall be cut to pieces in the morning." And the general drew aside the canvas, and there they saw him standing, and he said, "How many do you count me for?" He had won every battle that he had ever engaged in. He was the conqueror of conquerors. "How many do you count me for?" O souls, you have never counted Christ for what He is! You have put down your sins, but you have never counted what kind of a Christ He is who has come to save you. Rather do like Luther, who said that when the devil came to him, he brought him a long sheet containing a list of his sins, or of a great number of them, and Luther said to him, "Is that all?" "No," said the devil. "Well, go and fetch some more, then." Away went Satan to bring him another long list, as long as your arm. Said Luther, "Is that all?" "Oh, no!" said the devil, "I have more yet." "Well, go and bring them all," said Luther. "Fetch them all out, the whole list of them." Then it was a very long black list. I think that I have heard that it would have gone round the world twice. I know that mine would. Well, what did Luther say when he saw them all? He said, "Write at the bottom of them, 'The blood of Jesus Christ His Son cleanses us from all sin!'" It does not matter how long the list is when you write those blessed words at the end of it. The sins are all gone then. Did you ever take up from your table a bill for a large sum? You felt a kind of flush coming over your face. You looked down the list. It was a rather long list of items, perhaps from a lawyer or a builder. But when you looked at it, you saw that there was a penny stamp at the bottom, and that the account was receipted. "Oh!" you said, "I do not care how long it is; for it is all paid." So, though your sins are many, if you have a receipt at the bottom-if you have trusted Jesus-your sins are all gone, drowned in the Red Sea of your Savior's blood, and Christ is glorified in Your salvation. May God the Holy Spirit bring every unsaved one here tonight to repentance and faith in our Lord Jesus Christ! The Lord bless every one of you, for His name's sake! Amen.

JOHN 16. EXPOSITION BY C. H. SPURGEON:

Verse 1. These things have I spoken unto you, that you should not be offended.

The temptation is, when Christ is despised and rejected, for our hearts to begin to sink, and our faith to fail. Therefore did Christ warn His disciples that they "should not be offended."

2. They shall put you out of the synagogues: yes, the time comes, that whosoever kills you will think that he does God service.

The best of men are but men at the best, and they are very apt to fail when they find persecution hot against them, especially when even religious men, of a certain kind, count it to be a religious duty to persecute the people of God.

3. And these things will they do unto you, because they have not known the Father, nor Me.

This verse reminds us of our Lord's prayer on the cross, "Father, forgive them; for they know not what they do." Persecution of God's people usually arises from ignorance of God the Father and God the Son.

4. But these things have I told you, that when the time shall come, you may remember that I told you of them. And these things I said not unto you at the beginning, because I was with you.

"I was your Protector; by My personal presence, I so sustained your hearts that it did not matter what trouble you fell into; but now I am going away, and therefore I give you this warning."

5, 6. But now I go My way to Him that sent Me; and none of you asks Me, Where are You going? But because I have said these things unto you, sorrow has filled your heart.

We sometimes endure a needless sorrow, for which the asking of a single question might remove it. Our Lord says to His disciples, "If you knew where I was going, and understood My motive in going, your sorrow at My departure would be assuaged."

7. Nevertheless I tell you the truth; It is expedient for you that I go away: "It is for your profit to lose My personal presence, precious as that has been to you."

7. For if I go not away, the Comforter will not come unto you; but if I

depart, I will send Him unto you.

The word "Comforter" might just as well have been translated "Advocate." The Holy Spirit is that Divine Advocate who pleads the cause of God in us, and for us, and so comforts us. He it is who is now with us. If Jesus Christ were still upon earth in the flesh, He could only be in one place at one time. If He were in this assembly, He could not also be in Jerusalem or in New York; but the Comforter can be in all the gatherings of the Lord's people, and with each individual believer, the whole world over.

8-12. And when He is come, He will reprove the world of sin, and of righteousness, and of judgment: of sin, because they believe not on Me; of righteousness, because I go to My Father, and you see Me no more; of judgment, because the prince of this world is judged. I have yet many things to say unto you, but you cannot bear them now.

Teachers, learn wisdom from Christ. He did not try to teach His disciples everything at once; but, by teaching them one truth, He prepared them for another truth. Let us do the same with those whom we try to teach; let us dispense to them the simpler truths first, and afterwards those that are deeper and more mysterious.

13, 14. Howbeit when He the Spirit of truth is come, He will guide you into all truth: for He shall not speak of Himself; but whatsoever He shall hear, that shall He speak: and He will show you things to come. He shall glorify Me: for He shall receive of Mine, and shall show it unto you.

That spirit, which does not glorify Christ, is not the Spirit of God. Hereby shall you discern between the spirit of error and the Spirit of truth.

15, 16. All things that the Father has are Mine: therefore said I, that He shall take of Mine, and shall show it unto you. A little while, and you shall not see Me: and again a little while, and you shall see Me, because I go to the Father.

This is what our whole life is: "a little while." But in that little while there are little whiles of sadness, and little whiles of gladness-little whiles in which we have Christ with us, and little whiles in which we see Him, but find Him not. Blessed be God, we are going away from the land of these changing little whiles up to the Place where the sun shines in its strength forever and ever.

17, 18. Then said some of His disciples among themselves, What is this that He says unto us, A little while, and you shall not see Me: and, again, a little while, and you shall see Me: and, Because I go to the Father? They said therefore, What is this that He says, A little while? We cannot tell what He says.

Sometimes, when you are reading the Bible, you will come across a text of which you will say to yourselves, "What is this? We cannot tell what He says." But do not give up reading the Bible because you cannot understand it. There is a great deal that a father says which his child cannot comprehend, yet it is a part of the child's education to be with his father, and to hear some things that he does not at first understand; but, by and by, it all becomes clear. So, believer, what you know not now, you shall know hereafter.

19. Now Jesus knew that they were desirous to ask Him.

They did not ask Him, but they desired to do so, and a desire is a prayer. Where our blessed Master is present, the very desires of His people are prayers, even though their lips remain closed.

19, 20. And said unto them, Do you inquire among yourselves of that I said, A little while, and you shall not see Me: and again, a little while, and you shall see Me? Verily, verily, I say unto you, That you shall weep and lament, but the world shall rejoice: and you shall be sorrowful, but your sorrow shall be turned into joy. Oh, what a blessed promise!

21-24. A woman when she is in travail has sorrow, because her hour is come: but as soon as she is delivered of the child, she remembers no more the anguish, for joy that a man is born into the world. And you now therefore have sorrow: but I will see you again, and your heart shall rejoice, and your joy no man takes from you. And in that day you shall ask Me nothing. Verily, verily, I say unto you, Whatever you shall ask the Father in My name, He will give it you. Hitherto you have asked nothing in My name: Ask, and you shall receive, that your joy may be full.

They had asked very little, and they had never asked even that little in Christ's name; and there are but few Christians who do so even now. They ask for Christ's sake, which is a good plea, but to ask in Christ's name is better still-when you feel conscious that you have Christ's authority to use His name, you can put the King's own signature at the bottom of your petitions. There are some prayers to which a man dares not set Christ's seal; but when the prayer is such that Christ Himself might have offered it, then we may present it in His name, and we may be certain that we shall receive what we have asked.

25-28. These things have I spoken unto you in proverbs: but the time comes, when I shall no more speak unto you in proverbs, but I shall show you plainly of the Father. At that day you shall ask in My name: and I say not unto you that I will pray the Father for you: for the Father Himself loves you because you have loved Me, and have believed that I came out from God. I came forth from the Father, and am come into the world: again, I leave the world, and go to the Father.

Here are four unfathomable depths: "I came forth from the Father"-there is Christ's eternal pre- existence. "And am come into the world"-there is His incarnation. "Again, I leave the world,"-there is His death, resurrection, and ascension into the glory of God. "And go to the Father"-there is His exaltation to the Father's right hand."

29. His disciples said unto Him, Lo, now You speak plainly, and speak no proverb.

Did you never, when reading the Bible, come across a text, that was opened up to you so sweetly that you cried out just as these disciples did, "Lo, now You speak plainly, and speak no proverb"?

30, 31. Now are we sure that You know all things, and need not that any man should ask You: by this we believe that You came forth from God. Jesus answered them, Do you now believe?

Listen, you who imagine that you are so strong in faith, and every grace, that you think you are almost perfect: "Do you now believe?"

32. Behold, the hour comes, yes, is now come, that you shall be scattered, every man to his own, and shall leave Me alone:

Ah, me! These were the men who said they believed in Him; yet, in His time of trial, they fled like cowardly unbelievers. God help us, and sustain us, or we shall do as they did!

32, 33. And yet I am not alone, because the Father is with Me. These things I have spoken unto you, that in Me you might have peace. In the world you shall have tribulation: but be of good cheer; I have overcome the world.

Chapter 4
THE WORK OF THE HOLY SPIRIT

Are ye so foolish? having begun in the Spirit, are ye now made perfect by the flesh?"—Galatians 3:3.

Yes, we are just so foolish. Folly is bound up not only in the heart of a child, but in the heart of even a child of God; and though the rod may be said to bring folly out of a child, it will take many a repetition of the rod of affliction upon the shoulders of a Christian before that folly is taken out of him. I suppose we are all of us very sound as a matter of theory upon this point. If any should ask us how we hope to have our salvation worked in us, we should without the slightest hesitation aver our belief that salvation is of the Lord alone, and we should declare that, as the Holy Spirit first of all commenced our piety in us, we look alone to his might to continue and to preserve, and at last to perfect the sacred work. I say we are sound enough on that point as a matter of theory, but we are all of us very heretical and unsound as a matter of practice; for alas! you will not find a Christian who does not have to mourn over his self-righteous tendencies; you will not discover a believer who has not at certain periods in his life, to groan because the spirit of self-confidence has risen in his heart, and prevented him from feeling the absolute necessity of the Holy Spirit—has led him to put his confidence in the mere strength of nature, the strength of good intentions, the strength of strong resolutions, instead of relying upon the might of God the Holy Spirit alone. This one thing I know, brethren, that whilst as a preacher I can tell you all, that the Holy Spirit must work all our works in us, and that without him we can do nothing, yet as a man I find myself tempted to deny my own preachings, not in my words, but to deny them in fact by endeavoring to do deeds without looking first to the Holy Spirit. Whilst I should never be unsound in the didactic part of it, yet in that part which concerns the working of it out, in common with all that love the Lord Jesus, but who are still subject to the infirmities of flesh and blood, I have to groan that I repeatedly find myself, having begun in the Spirit, seeking to be made perfect in the flesh. Yes, we are just as foolish as that; and my brethren, it is well for us if we have a consciousness that we are foolish, for when a man is foolish and knows it, there is the hope that he will one day be wise: to know one's-self to be foolish is to stand upon the doorstep of the temple of wisdom; to understand the wrongness of any position is half way towards amending it; to be quite sure that our self-confidence is a heinous sin and folly, and an offense towards God, and to have that thought burned into us by God's Holy Spirit, is going a great length towards the absolute casting our self-confidence away, and the bringing of our souls in practice, as well as in theory, to rely wholly upon the power of God's Holy Spirit.

This evening, however, I shall run away from my text somewhat. Having just in a few words endeavored to explain the meaning of the whole sentence, I intend only this evening to dwell upon the doctrine which incidentally the apostle teaches us. He teaches us that we begin in the Spirit —"Having begun in the Spirit" I have already illustrated the whole text sufficiently for our understanding if God the Holy Spirit shall enlighten us; and I shall now, I say, confine myself to the thought that Christians begin in the Spirit; that the early part of Christianity is of God's Spirit, and of God's Spirit only, while it is equally true that all the way through we must lean upon the same power and depend upon the same strength. And I have selected this text for this reason: we have a very large influx of young believers, month after month—week after week I may say, for every week we receive additions to the church to a considerable number, and month after month these hands baptize into a profession of faith of the Lord Jesus many of those who are yet young in the faith of the Gospel. Now I am astonished to find those persons that thus come before me so well instructed in the doctrines of grace and so sound in all the truths of the covenant, insomuch that I may think it my boast and glory, in the name of Jesus, that I know not that we have any members, whom we have received into the church, who do not give their full assent and consent unto all the doctrines of the Christian religion, commonly called Calvinistic doctrines Those which men are wont to laugh at as being high doctrinal points, are those which they most readily receive, believe, and rejoice in. I find, however, that the greatest deficiency lies in this point, forgetfulness of the work of the Holy Spirit. I find them very easily remembering the work of God the Father; they do not deny the great doctrine of election; they can see clearly the great sentence of justification passed by the Father upon the elect through the vicarious sacrifice and perfect righteousness of Jesus; and they are not backward in understanding the work of Jesus either: they can see how Christ was the substitute for his people and stood in their room, place and stead; nor do they for one moment impugn any doctrine concerning God's Spirit; but they are not clear upon the point: they can talk upon the other points better than they can upon those which more particularly concern the blessed work of that all adorable person of the Godhead, God the Holy Spirit. I thought, therefore, that I would just preach as simply as ever I could upon the work of the Holy Spirit, and begin at the beginning; hoping on succeeding evening, at different times, as God the Holy Spirit shall guide me, to enter more fully into the subject of the work of the Spirit from the beginning even to the end. But let me say, it is no use your expecting me to preach a course of sermons. I know a great deal better than that. I don't believe God the Holy Spirit ever intended men to publish three months before hand, lists of sermons that they were going to preach; because there always will arise changes in Providence, and different states of mind both in the preacher and the hearer, and he will be a very wise man who has got an Old Moore's Almanack correct enough to let him know what would be the best sort of sermon to preach three months ahead. He had better leave it to his God to give him in the same hour what he shall speak, and look for his sermons, as the Israelites looked for the manna, day by day. However, we now commence by endeavoring to narrate the different points of the Spirit's work in the beginning of salvation.

And first, let me start by asserting that THE COMMENCEMENT OF SALVATION IS THE HOLY SPIRIT'S WORK. Salvation is not begun in the soul by the means of grace apart from the Holy Spirit. No man in the world is at liberty to neglect the means that God has appointed. If a house be builded for prayer, that man must expect no blessing who neglects to tread its floor. If a pulpit be erected for the ministration of the Word, no man must expect (although we do sometimes get more than we expect) to be saved except by the hearing of the Word. If the Bible be printed in our own native language, and we can read it, he who neglecteth Holy Scripture. and ceaseth from its study, has lost one great and grand opportunity of being blessed. There are many means of grace, and let us speak as highly of them as ever we can; we would be far from depreciating them; they are of the highest value; blessed are the people who have them; happy is the nation which is blessed with the means of grace. But my brethren, no man was ever saved by the means of grace apart from the Holy Spirit. You may hear the sermons of the man whom God delighteth to honor; ye may select from all your puritanical divines the writings of the man whom God did bless with a double portion of his Holy Spirit; ye may attend every meeting for prayer; ye may turn over the leaves of this blessed book; but in all this, there is no life for the soul apart from the breath of the Divine Spirit. Use these means, we exhort you to use them, and use them diligently: but recollect that in none of these means is there.anything that can benefit you unless God the Holy Spirit shall own and crown them. These are like the conduit pipes of the market place; when the fountain-head floweth with water then they are full, and we do derive a blessing from them; but if the stream be stayed, if the fountain head doth cease to give forth its current, then these are wells without water, clouds without rain; and ye may go to ordinances as an Arab turns to his skin bottle when it is dry, and with your parched lips ye may suck the wind and drink the whirlwind, but receive neither comfort, nor blessing, nor instruction, from the means of grace.

Nor is the salvation of any sinner commenced in him by a minister or by a priest, God forgive the man that ever called himself a priest, or suffered anyone else to call him so since the days of our Lord Jesus. The other morning at family prayer, I read the case of King Uzziah, who, having the kingly office, must needs thrust himself into the tabernacle of the Lord, and take the place of the priests. You remember how the priests withstood him, and said, "This is not thy portion, O Uzziah;" and you remember how he seized the censer and would burn incense as a priest before the Lord God; and whilst they yet spake, lo! the leprosy did rise in his face and he went out a leper, as white as snow, from the house of God. Ah! my brethren, it is no mean offense against God for any man to call himself a priest; not but that all the saints have a priestly office through Christ Jesus; but when any man putteth to the idea a speciality as applicable to himself above his fellows, and claimeth to be a priest among men, he committeth a sin before God, which, even though it be a sin of ignorance, is indeed great and grievous, and leadeth unto divers great and deadly errors, the guilt of which must lie partly upon the head of the man who gave foot-hold for those errors by allowing the title to be applied to himself. Well, there is no man—call him priest if you like, by way of ill courtesy—that can begin the work with us—no, not in the use of the ceremony. The Papist may tell us, and the Papist masked,—the devil in white, the Puseyite,—may tell us that grace begins in the heart at the dropping of the water upon the child's brow; but he telleth a lie, a lie before

God, that hath not even so much as the shadow of truth to justify the liar. There is no power in man, though he were ordained by one who could most assuredly claim succession from the apostles—though he were endowed with miraculous gifts, though he were the apostle Paul himself—if he did assert that he had in himself power to convert, power to regenerate, let him be accursed, for he hath denied the truth and Paul himself would have declared him anathema, maranatha, for having departed from the everlasting gospel, one cardinal point of which is—regeneration, the work of God the Holy Spirit; the new birth, a thing that is from above.

And, my brethren, it is quite certain that no man ever begins the new birth himself. The work of salvation never was commenced by any man. God the Holy Spirit must commence it. Now, the reasons why no man ever commenced the work of grace in his own heart, is very plain and palpable. First, because he cannot; secondly, because he won't. The best reason of all is, because he cannot—he is dead. Well the dead may be made alive, but the dead cannot make themselves alive, for the dead can do nothing. Besides, the new thing to be created as yet hath no being. The uncreated cannot create. "Nay," but you say, "that man can create." Yes, can hell create heaven? Then sin may create grace. What! will you tell me that fallen human nature, that has come almost to a level with the brutes, is competent to rival God; that it can emulate the divinity in working as great marvels, and in imparting as divine a life as even God himself can give? It cannot. Besides, it is a creation; we are created anew in Christ Jesus. Let any man create a fly, and afterwards let him create a new heart in himself; until he hath done the less he cannot do the greater. Besides, no man will. If any man could convert himself, there is no man that would. If any man saith he would, if that be true, he is already converted; for the will to be converted is in great part conversion. The will to love God, the desire to be in unison with Christ, is not to be found in any man who hath not already been brought to be reconciled with God through the death of his Son. There may be a false desire, a desire grounded upon a misrepresentation of the truth; but a true desire after true salvation by the true Spirit, is a certain index that the salvation already is there in the germ and in the bud, and only needs time and grace to develope itself. But certain it is, that man neither can nor will, being on the one hand utterly impotent and dead, and on the other hand utterly depraved and unwilling; hating the change when he sees it in others, and most of all despising it in himself. Be certain, therefore, that God the Holy

Spirit must begin, since none else can do so.

And now, my brethren, I must just enter into the subject very briefly, by showing what the Holy Spirit does in the beginning. Permit me to say that in describing the work, the true work of salvation in the soul, you must not expect me to exhibit any critical nicety of judgment. We have heard of an assembly of divines, who once debated whether men did repent first or believe first; and after a long discussion, some one wiser than the rest suggested another question, whether in the new-born child the lungs did first heave, or the blood did first circulate. "Now," said he, "when you shall ascertain the one, you may be able to ascertain the other." You shall not know which cometh first; they are, very likely, begotten in us at the same moment. We are not able, when we mention these things in order, exactly to declare and testify that these do all happen according to the order in which we mention them; but we only, according to the judgment of men, according to our own experience, seek now to set forth what is the usual way of acting with God the Holy Spirit in the work of salvation.

The first thing, then, that God the Holy Spirit doth in the soul is, to regenerate it. We must always learn to distinguish between regeneration and conversion. A man may be converted a great many times in his life, but regenerated only once. Conversion is a thing which is caused by regeneration, but regeneration is the very first act of God the Spirit in the soul. "What," say you, "does regeneration come before conviction of sin?" most certainly; there could be no conviction in the dead sinner. Now, regeneration quickens the sinner, and makes him live. He is not competent to have true spiritual conviction worked in him until, first of all he has received life. It is true that one of the earliest developments of life is conviction of sin; but before any man can see his need of a Saviour he must be a living man; before he can really, I mean, in a spiritual position, in a saving, effectual manner, understand his own deep depravity, he must have eyes with which to see the depravity, he must have ears with which to hear the sentence of the law, he must have been quickened and made alive; otherwise he could not be capable of feeling, or seeing, or discerning at all. I believe, then, the first thing the Spirit does is this—he finds the sinner dead in sin, just where Adam left him; he breathes into him a divine influence. The sinner knows nothing about how it is done, nor do any of us understand it. "Thou understandest not the wind—it bloweth where it listeth;" but we see its effects. Now, none of us can tell how the Holy Spirit works in men. I doubt not there have been some who have sat in these pews, and in the middle of a sermon or in prayer, or singing—they knew not how it was—the Spirit of God was in their hearts; he had entered into their souls; they were no longer dead in sin, no longer without thought, without hope, without spiritual capacity, but they had begun to live. And I believe this work of regeneration, when it is done effectually—and God the Spirit would not do it without doing it effectually—is done mysteriously, often suddenly, and it is done in divers manners; but still it hath always this mark about it—that the man although he may not understand how it is done, feels that something is done. The what, the how, he doth not know; but he knows that something is done; and he now begins to think thoughts he never thought before; he begins to feel as he never felt before; he is brought into a new state, there is a change wrought in him—as if a dead post standing in the street were on a sudden to find itself possessed of a soul, and did hear the sound of the passing carriages, and listen to the words of the foot-passengers; there is something quite new about it. The fact is, the man has got a spirit; he never had one before; he was nothing but a body and a soul; but now, God has breathed into him the third great principle, the new life, the Spirit, and he has become a spiritual man. Now, he is not only capable of mental exercise, but of spiritual exercise; as, having a soul before, he could repent, he could believe, as a mere mental exercise; he could think thoughts of God, and have some desires after him; but he could not have one spiritual thought, nor one spiritual wish or desire, for he had no powers that could educe these things; but now, in regeneration, he has got something given to him, and being given, you soon see its effects. The man begins to feel that he is a sinner; why did he not feel that before? Ah, my brethren, he could not, he was not in a state to feel; he was a dead sinner; and though he used to tell you, and tell God, by way of compliment, that he was a sinner, he did not know anything about it. He said he was a sinner; yes, but he talked about being a sinner just as the blind man talks about the stars that be has never seen, as he talks about the light, the existence of which he would not know unless he were told of it; but now it is a deep reality. You may laugh at him, ye who have not been regenerated; but now he has got something that really puts him beyond your laughter. He begins to feel the exceeding weight and evil of transgression; his heart trembles, his very flesh quivers—in some cases the whole frame is affected. The man is sick by day and night; his flesh creepeth on his bones for fear; he cannot eat, his appetite fails him. He cannot bear the sound of melody and mirth; all his animal spirits are dried up. He cannot rejoice; he is unhappy, he is miserable. downcast, distressed; in some cases, almost ready to go mad; though in the majority of cases it takes a lighter phase, and there are the gentle whispers of the Spirit; but even then, the pangs and pains caused by regeneration, while the new life discovers the sin and evil of the past condition of the man are things that are not to be well described or mentioned without tears. This is all the work of the Spirit.

And having brought the soul thus far, the next thing the Holy Spirit doth is, to teach the soul that it is utterly incapable of saving itself. It knew that before, mayhap, if the man sat under a Gospel ministry; but he only knew it with the ear, and understood it with the mind. Now, it has become part of his very life; he feels it; it has entered into his soul, and he knows it to be true. Once he thought he would be good, and thought that would save him; the Holy Spirit just knocks the brains out of that thought. "Then," he says, "I will try ceremonies. and see whether I cannot gain merit so;" God the Holy Spirit shoots the arrow right through the heart of that thought, and it falls dead before him, and he cannot bear the sight of the carcase, so that, like Abraham said of Sarah, he exclaims, "Bury the dead out of my sight." Though once he loved it dearly, now he hates the sight thereof. He thought once that he could believe; he had an Arminian notion in his head, that he could believe when he liked, and repent when he liked. Now, God the Spirit has brought him in such a condition, that he says, "I can do nothing." He begins to discover his own death, now that he is made alive; he did not know anything about it before. He now finds that he has no hand of faith to lift, though the minister tells him to do it. He now discovers, when he is bidden to pray, that he would, but cannot pray. He now finds that he is powerless, and he dies in the hand of God like clay in the hand of the potter, and is made to cry out, "O Lord, my God, unless thou save me, I am damned to all eternity; for I cannot lift a finger in this matter until thou first of all givest me strength." And if you urge him to do anything, he longs to be doing, but he is so afraid that it should only be fleshly doings, and not the doings of the Spirit, that he meditates, and stops, and stays, until he groans and cries; and feeling that these groans and cries are the real work of the Spirit, and prove that he has spiritual life, he then begins in right earnest to look to Jesus Christ the Saviour. But mark, all these things are by the Spirit, and none of them can ever be produced in the soul of any man or woman, apart from the divine influence of God the Holy Ghost.

This being done, the soul being now weaned from all confidence, and despairing and brought to its last standing place, yea, laid prostrate on the ground, the rope being about its neck, and the ashes and sackcloth on its head; God the Holy Ghost next applies the blood of Jesus to the soul, gives the soul the grace of faith whereby it lays hold of Jesus, and gives it an anointing of holy consolation and unction of assurance, whereby, casting itself wholly on the blood and righteousness of Jesus, it receiveth joy, knoweth itself to be saved, and rejoiceth in pardon. But mark, that is the work of the Spirit. Some preachers will tell their people, "Believe, only believe." Yes, it is right they should tell them so; but they should remember it is also right to tell them that even this must be the work of the Spirit; for though we say, "Only believe," that is the greatest only in the world; and what some men say is so easy is just what those who want to believe find to be the hardest thing in all the world. It is simple enough for a man that hath the Spirit in him to believe, when he hath the written Word before him and the witness of the Spirit in him; that is easy enough. But for the poor, tried sinner, who cannot see anything in the Word of God but thunder and threatening—for him to believe—ah my brethren, it is not such a little matter as some make it to be. It needs the fullness of the power of God's Spirit to bring any man to such faith as that.

Well, when the sinner hath thus believed, then the Holy Spirit bringeth all the precious things to him. There is the blood of Jesus; that can never save my soul, unless God the Spirit takes that blood, and sprinkles it upon my conscience. There is the perfect spotless righteousness of Jesus; it is a robe that will fit me and adorn me from head to foot, but it is no use to me till I have put it on; and I cannot put it on myself; God the Holy Spirit must put the robe of Jesus' righteousness on me. There is the covenant of adoption, whereby God gives me the privileges of a son; but I cannot rejoice in my adoption until I receive the spirit of adoption whereby I may be able to cry, "Abba, Father." So, beloved, you see—I might enlarge, but my time fails me —you see that every point that is brought out in the experience of the new-born Christian, every point in that part of salvation which we may call its beginning in the soul, has to do with God the Holy Spirit. There is no step that can be taken without him, there is nothing which can be accomplished aright without him; yea, though ye had the best of means, the rightest of ceremonies, the most orthodox of truths, and though ye did exercise, your minds upon all these things, and though the blood of Jesus Christ were shed for you, and God himself had ordained you from before the foundations of the world to be saved, yet still there must be that one link always inserted in the golden chain of the plan of salvation; for without that it were all incomplete. You must be quickened by the Spirit; you must be called out of darkness into light; you must be made a new creature in Christ Jesus.

Now, I wonder how many of you know anything about this. That is the practical part of it. Now my hearer, dost thou understand this? Perhaps, sir, thou art one exceeding wise, and thou turnest on thy heel with a sneer, and thou sayest "Supernaturalism in one of its phases; these Methodists are always talking about supernatural things." You are very wise, exceeding so, doubtless; but it seemeth to me that Nicodemus of old had gotten as far as you, and you have gotten no farther than he; for he asked "How could a man be born again when he is old?" And though every Sunday-school child has had a smile at the expense of Nicodemus's ignorance, you are not wiser. And yet you are a Rabbi, sir, and you would teach us, would you? And you would teach us about these things, and yet you sneer about supernaturalism. Well, the day may come—I pray it may come to you before the day of your death and your doom—when the Christ of the supernaturalists will be the only Christ for you; when you shall come into the floods of death, where you shall need something more than nature, then you will be crying for a work that is supernatural within your hearts; and it may be that then, when you first of all awake to know that your wisdom was but one of the methods of madness, you may perhaps have to cry in vain, having for your only answer, "I called, and ye refused; I stretched out my hands, and no man regarded; I also will mock at your calamity, and laugh when your fear cometh."

I hear another of you say, "Well, sir, I know nothing of this work of God the Holy Spirit, in my heart; I am just as good as other people, I never make a profession of religion; it is very rarely that I go into a place of worship at all, but I am as good as the saints, any of them: look at some of them—very fine fellows certainly." Stop, now, religion is a thing between yourself and your Maker, and you have nothing to do with those very fine fellows you have spoken of. Suppose I make a confession that a large number of those who are called saints deserve a great deal more to be called sinners double-dyed, and then white-washed,—suppose I make a confession of that, what has that to do with you? Your religion must be for yourself, and it must be between you and your God. If all the world were hypocrites, that would not exonerate you before your God. When you came before the Master, if you were still at enmity to him, could you venture to plead such an excuse as this—"All the world was full of hypocrites?" "Well," he would say, "what had that to do with you? so much the more reason why you should have been a honest man. If you say the church was thus drifting away upon the quicksands, through the evil conduct and folly of the members thereof, so much the more reason why you should have helped to make it sound, if you thought you could have done so." Another cries, "Well, I do not see that I need it; I am as moral a man as I can be; I never break the Sabbath; I am one of the most punctillious of Christians; I always go to church twice a Sabbath; I hear a thoroughly evangelical minister, and you would not find fault with him." Or perhaps says another, "I go to a Baptist chapel, I am always found there, I am scrupulously correct in my conduct; I am a good father, a good husband; I do not know that any man can find fault with me in business." Well certainly that is very good, and if you will be so good to-morrow morning as to go into Saint Paul's and wash one of those statues till you make it alive, then you will be saved by your morality; but since you, even you, are dead in trespasses and sins, without the Spirit you may wash yourself never so clean, but you cannot wash life into you any more than those statues, by all your washing, could be made to walk, or think, or breathe. You must be quickened by the Holy Spirit, for you are dead in trespasses and sins.

Yes, my comely maiden, thou that art everything excellent; thou that art not to be blamed in aught; thou that art affectionate, tender, kind, and dutiful; whose very life seems to be so pure, that all who see thee think thou seemest an angel; even thou, except thou be born again, canst not see the kingdom of God; the golden gate of heaven must grind upon its hinges with a doleful sound and shut thee out for ever, unless thou art the subject of a divine change, for this knows no exception. And, O ye vilest of the vile, ye who have wandered farthest from the paths of rectitude, "ye must be born again," ye must be quickened by a divine life; and it is comforting for you to recollect, that the very same power which can awaken the moral man, which can save the man of rectitude and honesty, is able to work in you, is able to change you; to turn the lion to a lamb, the raven to a dove.

O my hearers, ask yourselves, are you the subjects of this change? And if you be, rejoice with joy unspeakable, for happy is that mother's child. and full of glory, that can say, "I am born of God;" blessed is that man: God and the holy angels call him blessed who hath received the quickening of the

Spirit, and is born of God. For him there may be many troubles, but there is "a far more exceeding and eternal weight of glory" to counterbalance all his woe; for him there may be wars and fightings; but let him tarry, there are trumpets of victory, there are better wreaths than the laurels of conquerors, there is a crown of immortal glory, there is bliss unfading, there is acceptance in the breast of God for aye, and perpetual fellowship with Jehovah. But oh! if thou be not born again this night I can but tremble for thee, and lift my heart in prayer to God, and pray for thee, that he may now by his Divine Spirit make thee alive, give thee to know thy need of him, and then direct thee to the cross of Jesus. But if thou knowest thy need of a Saviour tonight, if thou art this night conscious of thy death in sin, hear me preach the gospel and I have done. The Lord Jesus Christ died for you. Dost thou know thyself to be guilty, not as the hypocrite pretendeth to know it, but dost thou know it consciously, sensitively, dost thou weep over it? Dost thou lament it? Dost thou feel that thou canst not save thyself? Art thou sick of all fleshly ways of saving? Canst thou say to-night, "Unless God shall put out the hand of his mercy, I know I deserve to be lost for ever, and I am?" Then, as the Lord my God liveth, before whom I stand, my Master bought you with his blood, and those whom he bought with blood he will have; from the fangs of the lion and the jaws of the bear will he pluck them. He will save thee, for thou art a part of his bloody purchase; he has taken thy sins upon his heal; he suffered in thy room and place, he has been punished for thee; thou shalt not die; "thy sins, which are many, are all forgiven," and I am the Master's glad herald to tell thee to night what his Word tells thee also, that thou mayest rejoice in the fullness of faith, for "Christ Jesus came into the world to save sinners," and "this is a faithful saying, and worthy of all acceptation"

May the Lord now be pleased to add his blessing for Jesus' sake.

Chapter 5
THE NECESSITY OF THE SPIRIT'S WORK

"And I will put my Spirit within you."—Ezekiel, 36:27.

The miracles of Christ are remarkable for one fact, namely that they are none of them unnecessary. The pretended miracles of Mahomet, and of the church of Rome, even if they had been miracles, would have been pieces of folly. Suppose that Saint Denis had walked with his head in his hand after it had been cut off, what practical purpose would have been subserved thereby? He would certainly have been quite as well in his grave, for any practical good he would have conferred on men. The miracles of Christ were never unnecessary. They are not freaks of power; they are displays of power it is true, but they all of them have a practical end. The same thing may be said of the promises of God. We have not one promise in the Scripture which may be regarded as a mere freak of grace. As every miracle was necessary, absolutely necessary, so is every promise that is given in the Word of God. And hence from the text that is before us, may I draw, and I think very conclusively, the argument, that if God in his covenant made with his people has promised to put his Spirit within them, it must be absolutely necessary that this promise should have been made, and it must be absolutely necessary also to our salvation that every one of us should receive the Spirit of God. This shall be the subject of this morning's discourse. I shall not hope to make it very interesting, except to those who are anxiously longing to know the way of salvation.

We start, then, by laying down this proposition—that the work of the Holy Spirit is absolutely necessary to us, if we would be saved.

I. In endeavoring to prove this, I would first of all make the remark that this is very manifest if we remember what man is by nature. Some say that man may of himself attain unto salvation—that if he hear the Word, it is in his power to receive it, to believe it, and to have a saving change worked in him by it. To this we reply, you do not know what man is by nature, otherwise you would never have ventured upon such an assertion. Holy

Scripture tells us that man by nature is dead in trespasses and sins. It does not say that he is sick, that he is faint, that he has grown callous, and hardened, and seared, but it says he is absolutely dead. Whatever that term "death" means in connection with the body, that it means in connection with man's soul, viewing it in its relation to spiritual things. When the body is dead it is powerless; it is unable to do any thing for itself; and when the soul of man is dead, in a spiritual sense, it must be, if there is any meaning in the figure, utterly and entirely powerless, and unable to do any thing of itself or for itself. When ye shall see dead men raising themselves from their graves, when ye shall see them unwinding their own sheets, opening their own coffin-lids, and walking down our streets alive and animate, as the result of their own power, then perhaps ye may believe that souls that are dead in sin may turn to God, may recreate their own natures, and may make themselves heirs of heaven, though before they were heirs of wrath. But mark, not till then. The drift of the gospel is, that man is dead in sin, and t at divine life is God's gift; and you must go contrary to the whole of that drift, before you can suppose a man brought to know and love Christ, apart from the work of the Holy Spirit. The Spirit finds men as destitute of spiritual life as Ezekiel's dry bones; he brings bone to bone, and fits the skeleton together, and then he comes from the four winds and breathes into the slain, and they live, and stand upon their feet, an exceeding great army, and worship God. But apart from that, apart from the vivifying influence of the Spirit of God, men's souls must lie in the valley of dry bones, dead, and dead for ever.

But Scripture does not only tell us that man is dead in sin; it tells us something worse than this, namely, that he is utterly and entirely averse to every thing that is good and right. "The carnal mind is enmity against God; for it is not subject to the law of God, neither indeed can be."—Romans 8:7. —Turn you all Scripture through, and you find continually the will of man described as being contrary to the things of God. What said Christ in that text so often quoted by the Arminian to disprove the very doctrine which it clearly states? What did Christ say to those who imagined that men would come without divine influence? He said, first, "No man can come unto me except the Father which hath sent me draw him;" but he said something more strong—"Ye will not come unto me that ye might have life." No man will come. Here lies the deadly mischief; not only that he is powerless to do good, but that he is powerful enough to do that which is wrong, and that his will is desperately set against every thing that is right. Go, Armenian, and tell your hearers that they will come if they please, but know that your Redeemer looks you in the face, and tells you that you are uttering a lie. Men will not come. They never will come of themselves. You cannot induce them to come; you cannot force them to come by all your thunders, nor can you entice them to come by all your invitations. They will not come unto Christ, that they may have life. Until the Spirit draw them, come they neither will, nor can.

Hence, then, from the fact that man's nature is hostile to the divine Spirit, that he hates grace, that he despises the way in which grace is brought to him, that it is contrary to his own proud nature to stoop to receive salvation by the deeds of another—hence it is necessary that the Spirit of God should operate to change the will, to correct the bias of the heart, to set man in a right track, and then give him strength to run in it. Oh! if ye read man and understand him, ye cannot help being sound on the point of the necessity of the Holy Spirit's work. It has been well remarked by a great writer, that he never knew a man who held any great theological error, who did not also hold a doctrine which diminished the depravity of man. The Armenian says man is fallen, it is true, but then he has power of will left, and that will is free; he can raise himself. He diminishes the desperate character of the fall of man. On the other hand, the Antinomian says, man cannot do any thing, but that he is not at all responsible, and is not bound to do it, it is not his duty to believe, it is not his duty to repent. Thus, you see, he also diminishes the sinfulness of man; and has not right views of the fall. But once get the correct view, that man is utterly fallen, powerless, guilty, defiled, lost, condemned, and you must be sound on all points of the great gospel of Jesus Christ. Once believe man to be what Scripture says he is—once believe his heart to be depraved, his affections perverted, his understanding darkened, his will perverse, and you must hold that if such a wretch as that be saved, it must e t e work of the Spirit of God, and of the Spirit of God alone.

2. I have another proof ready to hand. Salvation must be the work of the Spirit in us, because the means used in salvation are of themselves inadequate for the accomplishment of the work. And what are the means of salvation? Why, first and foremost stands the preaching of the Word of God. More men are brought to Christ by preaching than by any thing else; for it is God's chief and first instrument. This is the sword of the Spirit, quick and powerful, to the dividing asunder of the joints and marrow. "It pleaseth God by the foolishness of preaching to save them that believe." But what is there

in preaching, by which souls are saved, that looks as if it would be the means of saving souls? I could point you to divers churches and chapels into which you might step, and say, "Here is a learned minister, indeed, a man who would instruct and enlighten the intellect;" you sit down, and you say, "Well, if God means to work a great work, he will use a learned man like this." But do you know any learned men that are made the means of bringing souls to Christ, to any great degree? Go round your churches, if you please, and look at them, and then answer the question. Do you know any great men—men great in learning and wisdom—who have become spiritual fathers in our Israel? Is it not a fact that stares us in the face, that our fashionable preachers, our eloquent preachers, our learned preachers, are just the most useless men in creation for the winning of souls to Christ. And where are souls born to God? Why, in the house around which the jeer and the scoff and the sneer of the world have long gathered. Sinners are converted under the man whose eloquence is rough and homely, and who has nothing to commend him to his fellows, who has daily to fall on his knees and confess his own folly, and when the world speaks worst of him, feels that he deserves it all, since he is nothing but an earthen vessel, in which God is pleased to put his heavenly treasure. I will dare to say it, that in every age of the world the most despised ministry has been the most useful; and I could find you at this day poor Primitive Methodist preachers who can scarce speak correct English, who have been the fathers of more souls, and have brought to Christ more than any one bishop on the bench. Why, the Lord hath been pleased always to make it so, that he will clothe with power the weak and the foolish, but he will not clothe with power those who, if good were done, might be led to ascribe the excellence of the power to their learning, their eloquence, or their position. Like the apostle Paul, it is every minister's business to glory in his infirmities. The world says, "Pshaw! upon your oratory; it is rough, and rude, and eccentric." Yet, 'tis even so, but we are content, for God blesses it. Then so much the better that it has infirmities in it; for now shall it be plainly seen that it is not of man or by man, but the work of God, and of God alone. It is said that once upon a time a man exceedingly curious desired to see the sword with which a mighty hero had fought some desperate battles; casting his eye along the blade, he said, "Well, I don't see much in this sword." "Nay," said the hero, "but you have not examined the arm that wields it." And so when men come to hear a successful minister, they are apt to say, "I do not see any thing in him." No, but you have not examined the eternal arm that reaps its harvest with this sword of the Spirit. If ye had looked at the jaw-bone of the ass in Samson's hand, you would have said, "What! heaps on heaps with this!" No; bring out some polished blade; bring forth the Damascus steel! NO; but God would have all the glory, and, therefore, not with the polished steel, but with the jaw-bone must Samson get the victory. So with ministers; God has usually blessed the weakest to do the most good. Well, now, does it not follow from this, that it must be the work of the Spirit? Because, if there be nothing in the instrument that can lead thereunto, is it not the work of the Spirit when the thing is accomplished? Let me just put it to you. Under the ministry dead souls are quickened, sinners are made to repent, the vilest of sinners are made holy, men who came determined not to believe are compelled to believe. Now, who does this? If you say the ministry does it, then I say farewell to your reason, because there is nothing in the successful ministry which would tend thereunto. It must be that the Spirit worketh in man through the ministry or else such deeds would never be accomplished. You might as well expect to raise the dead by whispering in their ears, as hope to save souls by preaching to them, if it were not for the agency of the Spirit. Melancthon went out to preach, you know, without the Spirit of the Lord, and he thought he should convert all the people, but he found out at last that old Adam was too strong for young Melancthon, and he had to go back and ask for the help of the Holy Spirit or ever he saw a soul saved. I say, that the fact that the ministry is blessed proves, since there is nothing in the ministry, that salvation must be the work of a higher power.

Other means, however, are made use of to bless men's souls. For instance, the two ordinances of Baptism and the Lord's Supper. They are both made a rich means of grace. But let me ask you, is there any thing in baptism that can possibly bless any body? Can immersion in water have the slightest tendency to be blessed to the soul? And then with regard to the eating of bread and the drinking of wine at the Lord's Supper, can it by any means be conceived by any rational man that there is any thing in the mere piece of bread that we eat, or in the wine that we drink? And yet, doubtless, the grace of God does go with both ordinances for the confirming of the faith of those who receive them, and even for the conversion of those who look upon the ceremony. There must be something, then, beyond the outward ceremony; there must, in fact, be the Spirit of God, witnessing through the water, witnessing through the wine, witnessing through the bread, or otherwise none of these things could be means of grace to our souls. They could not edify; they could not help us to commune with Christ; they could not tend to the conviction of sinners, or to the establishment of saints. There must, then, from these facts, be a higher, unseen, mysterious influence—the influence of the divine Spirit of God.

3. Let me again remind you, in the third place, that the absolute necessity of the work of the Holy Spirit in the heart may be clearly seen from this fact, that all which has been done by God the Father, and all that has been done God the Son must be ineffectual to us, unless the Spirit shall reveal these things to our souls. We believe, in the first place, that God the Father elects his people; from before all worlds he chooses them to himself, but let me ask you—what effect does the doctrine of election have upon any man until the Spirit of God enters into him? How do I know whether God has chosen me from before the foundation of the world? How can I possibly knows. Can I climb to heaven and read the roll? Is it possible for me to force my way through the thick mists which hide eternity, and open the seven seals of the book, and read my name recorded there? Ah! no; election is a dead letter both in my consciousness and in any effect which it can produce upon me, until the Spirit of God calls me out of darkness into marvelous light. And then, through my calling, I see my election, and, knowing myself to be called of God, I know myself to have been chosen of God from before the foundation of the world. It is a precious thing—that doctrine of election—to a child of God. But what makes it precious? Nothing but the influence of the Spirit. Until the Spirit opens the eye to read, until the Spirit imparts the mystic secret, no heart can know its election. No angel ever revealed to any man that he was chosen of God; but the Spirit doth it. He, by his divine workings bears an infallible witness with our spirits that we are born of God; and then we are enabled to "read our title clear to mansions in the skies."

Look, again, at the covenant of grace. We know that there was a covenant made with the Lord Jesus Christ by his Father from before all worlds, and that in this covenant the persons of all his people were given to him, and were secured; but of what use, or of what avail is the covenant to us, until the Holy Spirit brings the blessings of the covenant to us? The covenant is, as it were, a holy tree laden with fruit; if the Spirit doth not shake that tree, and make the fruit fall therefrom, until it comes to the level of our standing, how can we receive it? Bring hither any sinner and tell him there is a covenant of grace, what is he advantaged thereby? "Ah," says he, "I may not be included in it; my name may not be recorded there; I may not be chosen in Christ;"

but let the Spirit of God dwell in his heart, richly by faith and love which is in Christ Jesus, and that man sees the covenant, ordered in all things and sure, and he cries with David, "It is all my salvation and all my desire."

Take, again, the redemption of Christ. We know that Christ did stand in the room, place, and stead of all his people, and that all those who shall appear in heaven will appear there as an act of justice as well as of grace, seeing that Christ was punished in their room and stead, and that it would have been unjust if God punished them, seeing that he had punished Christ for them. We believe that Christ, having paid all their debts, they have a right to their freedom in Christ—that Christ having covered them with his righteousness, they are entitled to eternal life as much as if they had themselves been perfectly holy. But of what avail is this to me, until the Spirit takes of the things of Christ and shows them to me? What is Christ's blood to any of you until you have received the Spirit of grace? You have heard the minister preach about the blood of Christ a thousand times, but you passed by; it was nothing to you that Jesus should die. You know that he did atone for sins that were not his own; but you only regarded it as a tale, perhaps, even an idle tale. But when the Spirit of God led you to the cross, and opened your eyes, and enabled you to see Christ crucified, ah, then there was something in the blood indeed. When his hand dipped the hyssop in the blood, and when it applied that blood to, your spirit, then there was a joy and peace in believing, such as you had never known before. But ah, my hearer, Christ's dying is nothing to thee unless thou hast a living Spirit within thee. Christ brings thee no advantage, saving, personal, and lasting, unless the Spirit of God hath baptized thee in the fountain filled with his blood, and washed thee from head to foot therein.

I only mention these few out of the many blessings of the covenant just to prove that they are, none of them, of any use to us, unless the Holy Spirit gives them to us. There hang the blessings on the nail—on the nail, Christ Jesus; but we are short of stature; we cannot reach them; the Spirit of God takes them down and gives them to us, and there they are; they are ours. It is like the manna in the skies, far out of mortal reach; but the Spirit of God opens the windows of heaven, brings down the bread, and puts it to our lips, and enables us to eat. Christ's blood and righteousness are like wine stored in the wine-vat; but we cannot get thereat. The Holy Spirit dips our vessel into this precious wine, and then we drink; but without the Spirit we must die and perish just as much, though the Father elect and the Son redeem, as though the Father never had elected, and though the Son had never bought us with his blood. The Spirit is absolutely necessary. Without him neither the works of the Father, nor of the Son, are of any avail to us.

4. This brings us to another point. The experience of the true Christian is a reality; but it never can be known and felt without the Spirit of God. For what is the experience of the Christian? Let me just give a brief picture of some of its scenes. There is a person come into this hall this morning—one of the most reputable men in London. He has never committed himself in any outward vice; he has never been dishonest; but he is known as a staunch, upright tradesman. Now, to his astonishment, he is informed that he is a condemned, lost sinner, and just as surely lost as the thief who died for his crimes upon the cross. Do you think that man will believe it? Suppose, however, that he does believe it, simply because he reads it in the Bible, do you think that man will ever be made to feel it? I know you say, "Impossible!" Some of you, even now, perhaps, are saying, "Well, I never should!" Can you imagine that honorable, upright tradesman, saying, "God be merciful to me, a sinner?"— standing side by side with the harlot and the swearer, and feeling in his own heart as if he had been as guilty as they were, and using just the same prayer and saying, "Lord, save, or I perish." You cannot conceive it, can you? It is contrary to nature that a man who has been so good as he should pat himself down among the chief of sinners. Ah! but that will be done before he will be saved; he must feel that before he can enter heaven. Now, I ask, who can bring him to such a leveling experience as that, but the Spirit of God? Ye know very well proud nature will not stoop to it. We are all aristocrats in our own righteousness; we do not like to bend down and come among common sinners. If we are brought there, it must be the Spirit of God who casts us to the ground. Why, I know if any one had told me that I should ever cry to God for mercy, and confess that I had been the vilest of the vile, I should have laughed in their face; I should have said, "Why I have not done anything particularly wrong; I have not hurt anybody." And yet I know this very day I can take my place upon the lowest form, and if I can get inside heaven I shall feel happy to sit among the chief of sinners, and praise that Almighty love which has saved even me from my sins.. Now, what works this humiliation of heart? Grace. It is contrary to nature for an honest and an upright man in the eye of the world to feel himself a lost sinner. It must be the Holy Spirit's work, or else it never will be done. Well, after a man has been brought here, can you conceive that man at last

conscience-stricken, and led to believe that his past life deserves the wrath of God? His first thought would be, "Well, now, I will live better than I ever have lived." He would say, "Now, I will try and play the hermit, and pinch myself here and there, and deny myself, and do penance; and in that way, by paying attention to the outward ceremonies of religion, together with a high moral character, I doubt not I shall blot out whatever slurs and stains there have been." Can you suppose that man brought at last to feel that, if ever he gets to heaven, he will have to get there through the righteousness of another? "Through the righteousness of another?" says he, "I don't want to be rewarded for what another man does,—not I. If I go there, I will go there and take my chance; I will go there through what I do myself. Tell me something to do, and I will do it; I will be proud to do it, however humiliating it may be, so that I may at last win the love and esteem of God." Now, can you conceive such a man as that brought to feel that he can do nothing?—that, good man as he thinks himself, he cannot do any thing whatever to merit God's love and favor; and that, if he goes to heaven, he must go through what Christ did? Just the same as the drunkard must go there through the merits of Christ, so this moral man must enter into life, having nothing about him but Christ's perfect righteousness, and being washed in the blood of Jesus. We say that this is so contrary to human nature, so diametrically opposed to all the instincts of our poor fallen humanity, that nothing but the Spirit of God can ever bring a man to strip himself of all self-righteousness, and of all creature strength, and compel him to rest and lean simply and wholly upon Jesus Christ the Saviour.

These two experiences would be sufficient to prove the necessity of the Holy Spirit to make a man a Christian. But let me now describe a Christian as he is after his conversion. Trouble comes, storms of trouble, and he looks the tempest in the face and says, "I know that all things work together for my good." His children die, the partner of his bosom is carried to the grave; he says, "The Lord gave and the Lord hath taken away, blessed be the name of the Lord." His farm fails, his crop is blighted; his business prospects are clouded, all seem to go, and he is left in poverty: he says, "Although the fig tree shall not blossom, neither shall fruit be in the vines; the labor of the olive shall fail and the fields shall yield no meat; the flocks shall be cut off from the fold, and there shall be no herd in the stalls: yet I will rejoice in the Lord, I will joy in the God of my salvation." You see him next laid upon a sick bed himself, and when he is there, he says, "It is good for me that I have been afflicted, for before I was afflicted I went astray, but now have I kept thy Word." You see him approaching at last the dark valley of the shadow of death, and you hear him cry, "Yea, though I walk through the valley of the shadow of death, I will fear no evil; thy rod and thy staff they comfort me, and thou thyself art with me." Now, I ask you, what makes this man calm in the midst of all these varied trials, and personal troubles, if it be not the Spirit of God? O, ye that doubt the influence of the Spirit, produce the like without him, go ye and die as Christians die, and live as they live, and if you can show the same calm resignation, the same quiet joy, and the same firm belief that adverse things shall, nevertheless, work together for good, then we may be, perhaps, at liberty to resign the point, and not till then. The high and noble experience of a Christian in times of trial and suffering, proves that there must be the operation of the Spirit of God.

But look at the Christian, too, in his joyous moments. He is rich. God has given him all his heart's desire on earth. Look at him: he says, "I do not value these things at all, except as they are the gift of God; I sit loose by them all and, notwithstanding this house and home, and all these comforts, 'I am willing to depart and be with Christ, which is far better.' It is true, I want nothing here on earth; but still I feel that to die would be gain to me, even though I left all these." He holds earth loosely; he does not grasp it with a tight hand, but looks upon it all as dust,—a thing which is to pass away. He takes but little pleasure therein, saying,—
"I've no abiding city here,
I seek a city out of sight."

Mark that man; he has plenty of room for pleasures in this world, but he drinks out of a higher cistern. His pleasure springs from things unseen; his happiest moments are when he can shut all these good things out, and when he can come to God as a poor guilty sinner, and come to Christ and enter into fellowship with him, and rise into nearness of access and confidence, and boldly approach to the throne of the heavenly grace. Now, what is it that keeps a man who has all these mercies from setting his heart upon the earth? This is a wonder, indeed, that a man who has gold and silver, and flocks and herds, should not make these his god, but that he should still say,—
"There's nothing round this spacious earth
That suits my large desire;
To boundless joy and solid mirth
My nobler thoughts aspire."

These are not my treasure; my treasure is in heaven, and in heaven only. What can do this? No mere moral virtue. No doctrine of the Stoic ever brought a man to such a pass as. that. No, it must be the work of the Spirit, and the work of the Spirit alone, that can lead a man to live in heaven, while there is a temptation to him to live on earth. I do not wonder that a poor man looks forward to heaven; he has nothing to look upon on earth. When there is a thorn in the nest, I do not wonder that the lark flies up, for there is no rest for him below. When you are beaten and chafed by trouble, no wonder you say,—

"Jerusalem! my happy home!
Name ever dear to me;
When shall my labors have an end,
In joy, and peace, and thee?"

But the greatest wonder is, if you line the Christian's nest never so softly, if you give him all the mercies of this life, you still cannot keep him from saying,—

"To Jesus, the crown of my hope,
My soul is in haste to be gone;
Oh bear me, ye cherubim, up,
And waft me away to his throne."

5. And now, last of all, the acts, the acceptable acts, of the Christian's life, cannot be performed without the Spirit; and hence, again, the necessity for the Spirit of God. The first act of the Christian's life is repentance. Have you ever tried to repent? If so, if you tried without the Spirit of God you know that to urge a man to repent without the promise of the Spirit to help him, is to urge him to do an impossibility. A rock might as soon weep, and a desert might as soon blossom, as a sinner repent of his own accord. If God should offer heaven to man, simply upon the terms of repentance of sin, heaven would be as impossible as it is by good works; for a man can no more repent of himself, than he can perfectly keep God's law; for repentance involves the very principle of perfect obedience to the law of God. It seems to me that in repentance there is the whole law solidified and condensed; and if a man can repent of himself then there is no need of a Saviour, he may as well go to heaven up the steep sides of Sinai at once.

Faith is the next act in the divine life. Perhaps you think faith very easy; but if you are ever brought to feel the burden of sin you would not find it quite so light a labor. If you are ever brought into deep mire, where there is no standing, it is not so easy to put your feet on a rock, when the rock does not seem to be there. I find faith just the easiest thing in the world when there is nothing to believe; but when I have room and exercise for my faith, then I do not find I have so much strength to accomplish it. Talking one day with a countryman, he used this figure: "In the middle of winter I sometimes think how well I could mow; and in early spring I think, oh! how I would like to reap; I feel just ready for it; but when mowing time comes, and when reaping time comes, I find I have not strength to spare." So when you have no troubles, couldn't you mow them down at once? When you have no work to do, couldn't you do it? But when work and trouble come you find how difficult it is. Many Christians are like the stag, who talked to itself, and said, "Why should I run away from the dogs? Look what a fine pair of horns I've got, and look what heels I've got too; I might do these hounds some mischief. Why not let me stand and show them what I can do with my antlers? I can keep off any quantity of dogs." No sooner did the dogs bark, than off the stag went. So with us. "Let sin arise," we say, "we will soon rip it up, and destroy it; let trouble come, we will soon get over it; but when sin and trouble come, we then find what our weakness is. Then we have to cry for the help of the Spirit; and through him we can do all things, though without him we can do nothing at all.

In all the acts of the Christian's life, whether it be the act of consecrating one's self to Christ, or the act of daily prayer, or the act of constant submission, or preaching the gospel, or ministering to the necessities of the poor, or comforting the desponding, in all these the Christian finds his weakness and his powerlessness, unless. he is clothed about with the Spirit of God. Why, I have been to see the sick at times, and I have thought how I would like to comfort them; and I could not get a word out that was worth their hearing, or worth my saying; and my soul has been in agony to be the means of comforting the poor, sick, desponding brother; but I could do nothing, and I came out of the chamber, and half wished I had never been to see a sick person in my life: I had so learned my own folly. So has it been full often in preaching. You get a sermon up, study it, and come and make the greatest mess of it that can possibly be. Then you say, "I wish I had never preached at all." But all this is to show us, that neither in comforting nor in preaching can one do any thing right, unless the Spirit work in us to will and to do of his own good pleasure. Every thing, moreover, that we do with out the Spirit is unacceptable to God; and whatever we do under his influence, however we may despise it, is not despised of God, for he never despises his own work, and the Spirit never can look upon what he works. in us with any other view than that of complacency and delight. If the Spirit helps me to groan, then God must accept the groaner. If thou couldst pray the best prayer in the world, without the Spirit, God would have nothing to do with it; but if thy prayer be broken, and lame, and limping, if the Spirit made it, God will look upon it, and say, as he did upon the works of creation, "It is very good;" and he will accept it.

And now let me conclude by asking this question. My hearer, then have you the Spirit of God in you? You have some religion, most of you, I dare say. Well, of what kind is it? Is it a homemade article? Did you make yourself what you are? Then, if so, you are a lost man up to this moment. If, my hearer, you have gone no further than you have walked yourself, you are not on the road to heaven yet; you have got your face turned the wrong way; but if you have received something which neither flesh nor blood could reveal to you, if you have been led to do the very thing which you once hated, and to love that thing which you once despised, and to despise that on which your heart and your pride were once set, then, soul, if this be the Spirit's work, rejoice; for where he hath begun the good work he will carry it on. And you may know whether it is the Spirit's work by this. Have you been led to Christ, and away from self: Have you been led away from all feelings, from all doings, from all willings, from all prayings, as the ground of your trust and your hope, and have you been brought nakedly to rely upon the finished work of Christ? If so, this is more than human nature ever taught any man; this is a height to which human nature never climbed. The Spirit of God has done that, and he will never leave what he has once begun, but thou shalt go from strength to strength, and thou shalt stand among the bloodwashed throng, at last complete in Christ, and accepted in the beloved. But if you have not the Spirit of Christ, you are none of his. May the Spirit lead you to your chamber now to weep, now to repent, and now to look to Christ, and may you now have a divine life implanted, which neither time nor eternity shall be able to destroy. God, hear this prayer, and send us away with a blessing, for Jesus' sake. Amen.

Chapter 6
THE HOLY SPIRIT'S INTERCESSION

"Likewise the Spirit also helpeth our infirmities: for we know not what we should what pray for as we ought: but the Spirit itself maketh intercession for us with groanings which cannot be uttered. And he that searcheth the hearts knoweth what is the mind of the Spirit, because he maketh intercession for the saints according the to will of God."
—Romans 8:26,27.

The APOSTLE PAUL was writing to a tried and afflicted people, and one of his objects was to remind them of the rivers of comfort which were flowing near at hand. He first of all stirred up their pure minds by way of remembrance as to their sonship,—for saith he "as many as are led by the Spirit of God, they are the sons of God." They were, therefore, encouraged to take part and lot with Christ, the elder brother, with whom they had become joint heirs; and they were exhorted to suffer with him, that they might afterwards be glorified with him. All that they endured came from a Father's hand, and this should comfort them. A thousand sources of joy are opened in that one blessing of adoption. Blessed be the God and Father of our Lord Jesus Christ, by whom we have been begotten into the family of grace.

When Paul had alluded to that consoling subject he turned to the next ground of comfort—namely, that we are to be sustained under present trial by hope. There is an amazing glory in reserve for us, and though as yet we cannot enter upon it, but in harmony with the whole creation must continue to groan and travail, yet the hope itself should minister strength to us, and enable us patiently to bear "these light afflictions, which are but for a moment." This also is a truth full of sacred refreshment: hope sees a crown in reserve, mansions in readiness, and Jesus himself preparing a place for us, and by the rapturous sight she sustains the soul under the sorrows of the hour. Hope is the grand anchor by whose means we ride out the present storm.

The apostle then turns to a third source of comfort, namely, the abiding of the Holy Spirit in and with the Lord's people. He uses the word "likewise" to intimate that in the same manner as hope sustains the soul, so does the Holy Spirit strengthen us under trial. Hope operated spiritually upon our spiritual faculties, and so does the Holy Spirit, in some mysterious way, divinely operate upon the new-born faculties of the believer, so that he is sustained under his infirmities. In his light shall we see light: I pray, therefore, that we may be helped of the Spirit while we consider his mysterious operations, that we may not fall into error or miss precious truth through blindness of heart.

The text speaks of "our infirmities," or as many translators put it in the singular—of "our infirmity." By this is intended our affliction, and the weakness which trouble discovers in us. The Holy Spirit helps us to bear the infirmity of our body and of our mind; he helps us to bear our cross, whether it be physical pain, or mental depression, or spiritual conflict, or slander, or poverty, or persecution. He helps our infirmity; and with a helper so divinely strong we need not fear for the result. God's grace will be sufficient for us; his strength will be made perfect in weakness.

I think, dear friends, you will all admit that if a man can pray, his trouble is at once lightened. When we feel that we have power with God and can obtain anything we ask for at his hands, then our difficulties cease to oppress us. We take our burden to our heavenly Father and tell it out in the accents of childlike confidence, and we come away quite content to bear whatever his holy will may lay upon us. Prayer is a great outlet for grief; it draws up the sluices, and abates the swelling flood, which else might be too strong for us. We bathe our wound in the lotion of prayer, and the pain is lulled, the fever is removed. We may be brought into such perturbation of mind, and perplexity of heart, that we do not know how to pray. We see the mercy-seat, and we perceive that God will hear us: we have no doubt about that, for we know that we are his own favoured children, and yet we hardly know what to desire. We fall into such heaviness of spirit, and entanglement of thought, that the one remedy of prayer, which we have always found to be unfailing, appears to be taken from us. Here, then, in the nick of time, as a very present help in time of trouble, comes in the Holy Spirit. He draws near to teach us how to pray, and in this way he helps our infirmity, relieves our suffering, and enables us to bear the heavy burden without fainting under the load.

At this time our subjects for consideration shall be, firstly, the help which the Holy Spirit gives; secondly, the prayers which he inspires; and thirdly, the success which such prayers ore certain to obtain.

I. First, then, let us consider THE HELP WHICH THE HOLY GHOST GIVES.

The help which the Holy Ghost renders to us meets the weakness which we deplore. As I have already said, if in time of trouble a man can pray, his burden loses its weight. If the believer can take anything and everything to God, then he learns to glory in infirmity, and to rejoice in tribulation; but sometimes we are in such confusion of mind that we know not what we should pray for as we ought. In a measure, through our ignorance, we never know what we should pray for until we are taught of the Spirit of God, but there are times when this beclouding of the soul is dense indeed, and we do not even know what would help us out of our trouble if we could obtain it. He see the disease, but the name of the medicine is not known to us. We look over the many things which we might ask for of the Lord, and we feel that each of them would be helpful, but that none of them would precisely meet our case. For spiritual blessings which we know to be according to the divine will we could ask with confidence, but perhaps these would not meet our peculiar circumstances. There are other things for which we are allowed to ask, but we scarcely know whether, if we had them, they would really serve our turn, and we also feel a diffidence as to praying for them. In praying for temporal things we plead with measured voices, ever referring our petition for revision to the will of the Lord. Moses prayed that he might enter Canaan, but God denied him; and the man that was healed asked our Lord that he might be with him, but he received for answer, "Go home to thy friends." We pray evermore on such matters with this reserve, "Nevertheless, not as I will, but as thou wilt." At times this very spirit of resignation appears to increase our spiritual difficulty, for we do not wish to ask for anything that would be contrary to the mind of God and yet we must ask for something. We are reduced to such straits that we must pray, but what shall be the particular subject of prayer we cannot for a while make out. Even when ignorance and perplexity are removed, we know not what we should pray for "as we ought." When we know the matter of prayer, we yet fail to pray in a right manner. We ask, but we are afraid that we shall not have, because we do not exercise the thought, or the faith, which we judge to be essential to prayer. We cannot at times command even the earnestness which is the life of supplication: a torpor steals over us, our heart is chilled, our hand is numbed, and we cannot wrestle with the angel. We know what to pray for as to objects, but we do not know what to pray for "as we ought" it is the manner of the prayer which perplexes us, even when the matter is decided upon. How can I pray? My mind wanders: I chatter like a crane; I roar like a beast in pain; I moan in the brokenness of my heart, but oh, my God, I know not what it is my inmost spirit needs; or if I know it, I know not how to frame my petition aright before thee. I know not how to open my lips in thy majestic presence: I am so troubled that I cannot speak. My spiritual distress robs me of the power to pour out my heart before my God. Now, beloved, it is in such a plight as this that the Holy Ghost aids us with his divine help, and hence he is "a very present help in time of trouble."

Coming to our aid in our bewilderment he instructs us. This is one of his frequent operations upon the mind of the believer: "he shall teach you all things." He instructs us as to our need, and as to the promises of God which refer to that need. He shows us where our deficiencies are, what our sins are, and what our necessities are; he sheds a light upon our condition, and makes us feel deeply our helplessness, sinfulness, and dire poverty; and then he casts the same light upon the promises of the Word, and lays home to the heart that very text which was intended to meet the occasion—the precise promise which was framed with foresight of our present distress. In that light he makes the promise shine in all its truthfulness, certainty, sweetness, and suitability, so that we, poor trembling sons of men, dare take that word into our mouth which first came out of God's mouth, and then come with it as an argument, and plead it before the throne of the heavenly grace. Our prevalence in prayer lies in the plea, "Lord, do as thou hast said." How greatly we ought to value the Holy Spirit, because when we are in the dark he gives us light, and when our perplexed spirit is so befogged and beclouded that it cannot see its own need, and cannot find out the appropriate promise in the Scriptures, the Spirit of God comes in and teaches us all things, and brings all things to our remembrance, whatsoever our Lord has told us. He guides us in prayer, and thus he helps our infirmity.

But the blessed Spirit does more than this, he will often direct the mind to the special subject of prayer. He dwells within us as a counsellor, and points out to us what it is we should seek at the hands of God. We do not know why it is so, but we sometimes find our minds carried as by a strong under current into a particular line of prayer for some one definite object. It is not merely that our judgment leads us in that direction, though usually the Spirit of God acts upon us by enlightening our judgment, but we often feel an unaccountable and irresistible desire rising again and again within our heart, and this so presses upon us, that we not only utter the desire before God at our ordinary times for prayer, but we feel it crying in our hearts all the day long, almost to the supplanting of all other considerations. At such times we should thank God for direction and give our desire a clear road: the Holy Spirit is granting us inward direction as to how we should reckon upon good success in our pleadings. Such guidance will the Spirit give to each of you if you will ask him to illuminate you. He will guide you both negatively and positively. Negatively, he will forbid you to pray for such and such a thing, even as Paul essayed to go into Bithynia, but the Spirit suffered him not: and, on other hand, he will cause you to hear a cry within your soul which shall guide your petitions, even as he made Paul hear the cry from Macedonia, saying, "Come over and help us." The Spirit teaches wisely, as no other teacher can do. Those who obey his promptings shall not walk in darkness. He leads the spiritual eye to take good and steady aim at the very centre of the target, and thus we hit the mark in our pleadings.

Nor is this all, for the spirit of God is not sent merely to guide and help our devotion, but he himself "maketh intercession for us" according to the will of God. By this expression it cannot be meant that the Holy Spirit ever groans or personally prays; but that he excites intense desire and created unutterable groanings in us, and these are ascribed to him. Even as Solomon built the temple because he superintended and ordained all, and yet I know not that he ever fashioned a timber or prepared a stone, so doth the Holy Spirit pray and plead within us by leading us to pray and plead. This he does by arousing our desires. The Holy Spirit has a wonderful power over renewed hearts, as much power as the skillful minstrel hath over the strings among which he lays his accustomed hand. The influences of the Holy Ghost at times pass through the soul like winds through an Eolian harp, creating and inspiring sweet notes of gratitude and tones of desire, to which we should have been strangers if it had not been for his divine visitation. He can arouse us from our lethargy, he can warm us out of our lukewarmness, he can enable us when we are on our knees to rise above the ordinary routine of prayer into that victorious importunity against which nothing can stand. He can lay certain desires so pressingly upon our hearts that we can never rest till they are fulfilled. He can make the zeal for God's house to eat us up, and the passion for God's glory to be like a fire within our bones; and this is one part of that process by which in inspiring our prayers he helps our infirmity.

True Advocate is he, and Comforter most effectual. Blessed be his name.

The Holy Spirit also divinely operates in the strengthening of the faith of believers. That faith is at first of his creating, and afterwards it is of his sustaining and increasing: and oh, brothers and sisters, have you not often felt your faith rise in proportion to your trials? Have you not, like Noah's ark, mounted towards heaven as the flood deepened around you? You have felt as sure about the promise as you felt about the trial. The affliction was, as it were, in your very bones, but the promise was also in your very heart. You could not doubt the affliction, for you smarted under it, but you might almost as soon have doubted the divine help, for your confidence was firm and unmoved. The greatest faith is only what God has a right to expect from us, yet do we never exhibit it except as the Holy Ghost strengthens our confidence, and opens up before us the covenant with all its seals and securities. He it is that leads our soul to cry, "though my house be not so with God, yet hath he made with me an everlasting covenant ordered in all things and sure." Blessed be the Divine Spirit then, that since faith is essential to prevailing prayer, he helps us in supplication by increasing our faith. Without faith prayer cannot speed, for he that wavereth is like a wave of the sea driven with the wind and tossed, and such an one may not expect anything of the Lord; happy are we when the Holy Spirit removes our wavering, and enables us like Abraham to believe without staggering, knowing full well that he who has promised is able also to perform.

By three figures I will endeavour to describe the work of the Spirit of God in this matter, though they all fall short, and indeed all that I can say must fall infinitely short of the glory of his work. The actual mode of his working upon the mind we may not attempt to explain; it remains a mystery, and it would be an unholy intrusion to attempt to remove the veil. There is no difficulty in our believing that as one human mind operates upon another mind, so does the Holy Spirit influence our spirits. We are forced to use words if we would influence our fellow-men, but the Spirit of God can operate upon the human mind more directly, and communicate with it in silence. Into that matter, however, we will not dive lest we intrude where our knowledge would be drowned by our presumption.

My illustrations do not touch the mystery, but set forth the grace. The Holy Spirit acts to his people somewhat as a prompter to a reciter. A man has to deliver a piece which he has learned; but his memory is treacherous, and therefore somewhere out of sight there is a prompter, so that when the speaker is at a loss and might use a wrong word, a whisper is heard, which suggests the right one. When the speaker has almost lost the thread of his discourse he turns his ear, and the prompter gives him the catch-word and aids his memory. If I may be allowed the simile, I would say that this represents in part the work of the Spirit of God in us,—suggesting to us the right desire, and bringing all things to our remembrance whatsoever Christ has told us. In prayer we should often come to a dead stand, but he incites, suggests, and inspires, and so we go onward. In prayer we might grow weary, but the Comforter encourages and refreshes us with cheering thoughts. When, indeed, we are in our bewilderment almost driven to give up prayer, the whisper of his love drops a live coal from off the altar into our soul, and our hearts glow with greater ardour than before. Regard the Holy Spirit as your prompter, and let your ear be opened to his voice.

But he is much more than this. Let me attempt a second simile: he is as an advocate to one in peril at law. Suppose that a poor man had a great law-suit, touching his whole estate, and he was forced personally to go into court and plead his own cause, and speak up for his rights. If he were an uneducated man he would be in a poor plight. An adversary in the court might plead against him, and overthrow him, for he could not answer him. This poor man knows very little about law, and is quite unable to meet his cunning opponent. Suppose one who was perfect in the law should take up his cause warmly, and come and live with him, and use all his knowledge so as to prepare his case for him, draw up his petitions for him, and fill his mouth with arguments,—would not that be a grand relief? This counsellor would suggest the line of pleading, arrange the arguments, and put them into right courtly language. When the poor man was baffled by a question asked in court, he would run home and ask his adviser, and he would tell him exactly how to meet the objector. Suppose, too, that when he had to plead with the judge himself, this advocate at home should teach him how to behave and what to urge, and encourage him to hope that he would prevail,—would not this be a great boon? Who would be the pleader in such a case? The poor client would plead, but still, when he won the suit, he would trace it all to the advocate who lived at home, and gave him counsel: indeed, it would be the advocate pleading for him, even while he pleaded himself. This is an instructive emblem of a great fact. Within this narrow house of my body, this tenement of clay, if I be a true believer, there dwells the Holy Ghost, and when I desire to pray I may ask him what I should pray for as I ought, and he will help me. He will write the prayers which I ought to offer upon the tablets of my heart, and I shall see them there, and so I shall be taught how to plead. It will be the Spirit's own self pleading in me, and by me, and through me, before the throne of grace. What a happy man in his law-suit would such a poor man be, and how happy are you and I that we have the Holy Ghost to be our Counsellor!

Yet one more illustration: it is that of a father aiding his boy. Suppose it to be a time of war centuries back. Old English warfare was then conducted by bowmen to a great extent. Here is a youth who is to be initiated in the art of archery, and therefore he carries a bow. It is a strong bow, and therefore very hard to draw; indeed, it requires more strength than the urchin can summon to bend it. See how his father teaches him. "Put your right hand here, my boy, and place your left hand so. Now pull"; and as the youth pulls, his father's hands are on his hands, and the bow is drawn. The lad draws the bow: ay, but it is quite as much his father, too. We cannot draw the bow of prayer alone. Sometimes a bow of steel is not broken by our hands, for we cannot even bend it; and then the Holy Ghost puts his mighty hand over ours, and covers our weakness so that we draw; and lo, what splendid drawing of the bow it is them! The bow bends so easily we wonder how it is; away flies the arrow, and it pierces the very center of the target, for he who giveth have won the day, but it was his secret might that made us strong, and to him be the glory of it.

Thus have I tried to set forth the cheering fact that the Spirit helps the people of God.

II. Our second subject is THE PRAYER WHICH THE HOLY SPIRIT INSPIRES, or that part of prayer which is especially and peculiarly the work of the Spirit of God. The text says, "The Spirit itself maketh intercession for us with groanings which cannot be uttered." It is not the Spirit that groans, but we that groan; but as I have shown you, the Spirit excited the emotion which causes us to groan.

It is clear then the prayers which are indited in us by the spirit of God are those which arise from our inmost soul. A man's heart is moved when he groans. A groan is a matter about which there is no hypocrisy. A groan cometh not from the lips, but from the heart. A groan then is a part of prayer which we owe to the Holy Ghost, and the same is true of all the prayer which wells up from the deep fountains of our inner life. The prophet cried, "My bowels, my bowels, I am pained at my very heart: my heart maketh a noise in me." This deep ground-swell of desire, this tidal motion of the life-floods is caused by the Holy Spirit. His work is never superficial, but always deep and inward.

Such prayers will rise within us when the mind is far too troubled to let us speak. We know not what we should pray for as we ought, and then it is that we groan, or utter some other inarticulate sound. Hezekiah said, "like a crane or a swallow did I chatter." The psalmist said, "I am so troubled that I cannot I have roared by reason of the disquietness of my heart"; but he added, "Lord, all my desire is before thee; and my groaning is not hid from thee." The sighing of the prisoner surely cometh up into the ears of the Lord. There is real prayer in these "groanings that cannot be uttered." It is the power of the Holy Ghost in us which creates all real prayer, even that which takes the form of a groan because the mind is incapable, by reason of its bewilderment and grief, of clothing its emotion in words. I pray you never think lightly of the supplications of your anguish. Rather judge that such prayers are like Jabez, of whom it is written, that "he was more honourable than his brethren, because his mother bare him with sorrow." That which is thrown up from the depth of the soul, when it is stirred with a terrible tempest, is more precious than pearl or coral, for it is the intercession of the Holy Spirit.

These prayers are sometimes "groanings that cannot be uttered," because they concern such great things that they cannot be spoken. I want, my Lord! I want, I want; I cannot tell thee what I want: but I seem to want all things. If it were some little thing, my narrow capacity could comprehend and describe it, but I need all covenant blessings. Thou knowest what I have need of before I ask thee, and though I cannot go into each item of my need, I know it to be very great, and such as I myself can never estimate. I groan, for I can do no more. Prayers which are the offspring of great desires, sublime aspirations, and elevated designs are surely the work of the Holy Spirit, and their power within a man is frequently so great that he cannot find expression for them. Words fail, and even the sighs which try to embody them cannot be uttered.

But it may be, beloved, that we groan because we are conscious of the littleness of our desire, and the narrowness of our faith. The trial, too. may seem too mean to pray about. I have known what it is to feel as if I could not pray about a certain matter, and yet I have been obliged to groan about it. A thorn in the flesh may be as painful a thing as a sword in the bones, and yet we may go and beseech the Lord thrice about it, and getting no answer we may feel that we know not what to pray for as we ought; and yet it makes us groan. Yes, and with that natural groan there may go up an unutterable groaning of the Holy Spirit. Beloved, what a different view of prayer God has from that which men think to be the correct one. You may have seen very beautiful prayers in print, and you may have heard very charming compositions from the pulpit, but I trust you have not fallen in love with them. Judge these things rightly. I pray you never think well of fine prayers, for before the thrice holy God it ill becomes a sinful suppliant to play the orator. We heard of a certain clergyman who was said to have given forth "the finest prayer ever offered to a Boston audience." Just so! The Boston audience received the prayer, and there it ended. We want the mind of the spirit in prayer, and not he mind of the flesh. The tail feathers of pride should be pulled out of our prayers, for they need only the wing feathers of faith; the peacock feathers of poetical expression are out of place before the throne of God. Hear me, what remarkably beautiful language he used in prayer!" "What an intellectual treat his prayer was! Yes, yes; but God looks at the heart. To him fine language is as sounding brass or tinkling cymbal, but a groan has music in it. We do not like groans: our ears are much too delicate to tolerate such dreary sounds; but not so the great Father of spirits. A Methodist brother cries, "Amen," and you say, "I cannot bear such Methodistic noise"; no, but if it comes from the man's heart God can bear it. When you get upstairs into your chamber this evening to pray, and find you cannot pray, but have to moan out, "Lord, I am too full of anguish and too perplexed to pray, hear thou the voice of my roaring," though you reach to nothing else you will be really praying. When like David we can say, "I opened my mouth and panted," we are by no means in an ill state of mind. All fine language in prayer, and especially all intoning or performing of prayers, must be abhorrent to God; it is little short of profanity to offer solemn supplication to God after the manner called "intoning." The sighing of a true heart is infinitely more acceptable, for it is the work of the Spirit of God.

   We may say of the prayers which the Holy Spirit works in us that they are prayers of knowledge. Notice, our difficulty is that we know not what we should pray for; but the Holy Spirit does know, and therefore he helps us by enabling us to pray intelligently, knowing what we are asking for, so far as this knowledge is needful to valid prayer. The text speaks "of the mind of the Spirit." What a mind that must be!—the mind of that Spirit who arranged all the order which now pervades this earth! There once was chaos and confusion, but the Holy Spirit brooded over all, and His mind is the originator of that beautiful arrangement which we so admire in the visible creation. What a mind his must be! The Holy Spirit's mind is seen in our intercessions when under his sacred influence we order our case before the Lord, and plead with holy wisdom for things convenient and necessary. What wise and admirable desires must those be which the Spirit of Wisdom himself works in us!

Moreover, the Holy Spirit's intercession creates prayers offered in a proper manner. I showed you that the difficulty is that we know not what we should pray for "as we ought," and the Spirit meets that difficulty by making intercession for us in a right manner. The Holy Spirit works in us humility, earnestness, intensity, importunity, faith, and resignation, and all else that is acceptable to God in our supplications. We know not how to mingle these sacred spices in the incense of prayer. We, if left to ourselves at our very best, get too much of one ingredient or another, and spoil the sacred compound, but the Holy Spirit's intercessions have in them such a blessed blending of all that is good that they come up as a sweet perfume before the Lord. Spirit-taught prayers are offered as they ought to be. They are his own intercession in some respects, for we read that the Holy Spirit not only helps us to intercede but "maketh intercession." It is twice over declared in our text that he maketh intercession for us; and the meaning of this I tried to show when I described a father as putting his hands upon his child's hands. This is something more than helping us to pray, something more than encouraging us or directing us,—but I venture no further, except to say that he puts such force of his own mind into our poor weak thoughts and desires and hopes, that he himself maketh intercession for us, working in us to will and to pray according to his good pleasure.

I want you to notice, however, that these intercessions of the Spirit are only in the saints. "He maketh intercession for us," and "He maketh intercession for the saints." Does he do nothing for sinners, then? Yes, he quickens sinners into spiritual life, and he strives with them to overcome their sinfulness and turn them into the right way; but in the saints he works with us and enables us to pray after his mind and according to the will of God. His intercession is not in or for the unregenerate. O, unbelievers you must first be made saints or you cannot feel the Spirit's intercession within you. What need we have to go to Christ for the blessing of the Holy Ghost, which is peculiar to the children of God, and can only be ours by faith in Christ Jesus! "To as man as received him to them gave he power to become the sons of God"; and to the sons of God alone cometh the Spirit of adoption, and all his helping grace. Unless we are the sons of God the Holy Spirit's indwelling shall not be ours: we are shut out from the intercession of the Holy Ghost, ay, and from the intercession of Jesus too, for he hath said, "I pray not for the world, but for them which thou hast given me."

Thus I have tried to show you the kind of prayer which the Spirit inspires.

III. Our third and last point is THE SURE SUCCESS OF ALL SUCH PRAYERS.

All the prayers which the Spirit of God inspires in us must succeed, because, first, there is a meaning in them which God reads and approves. When the Spirit of God writes a prayer upon a man's heart, the man himself may be in such a state of mind that he does not altogether know what it is. His interpretation of it is a groan, and that is all. Perhaps he does not even get so far as that in expressing the mind of the Spirit, but he feels greenings which he cannot utter, he cannot find a door of utterance for his inward grief. Yet our heavenly Father, who looks immediately upon the heart, reads what the Spirit of God has indited there, and does not need even our groans to explain the meaning. He reads the heart itself: "he knoweth,' says the text, "what is the mind of the Spirit." The Spirit is one with the Father, and the Father knows what the Spirit means. The desires which the Spirit prompts may be too spiritual for such babes in grace as we are actually to describe or to express, and yet the Spirit writes the desire on the renewed mind, and the Father sees it. Now that which God reads in the heart and approves of—for the word to "know" in this case includes approval as well as the mere act of omniscience—what God sees and approves of in the heart must succeed. Did not Jesus say, "Your heavenly Father knoweth that you have need of these things before you ask them"? Did he not tell us this as an encouragement to believe that we shall receive all needful blessings? So it is with those prayers which are all broken up, wet with tears, and discordant with those sighs and inarticulate expressions and heavings of the bosom, and sobbings of the heart and anguish and bitterness of spirit, our gracious Lord reads them as a man reads a book, and they are written in a character which he fully understands. To give a simple figure: if I were to come into your house I might find there a little child that cannot yet speak plainly. It cries for something, and it makes very odd and objectionable noises, combined with signs and movements, which are almost meaningless to stranger, but his mother understands him, and attends to his little pleadings. A mother can translate baby-talk: she comprehends incomprehensible noises. Even so doth our Father in heaven know all about our poor baby talk, for our prayer is not much better. He knows and comprehends the cryings, and meanings, and sighings, and chatterings of his bewildered children. Yea, a tender mother knows her child's needs before the child knows what it wants. Perhaps the little one stutters, stammers, and cannot get its words out, but the mother sees what he would say, and takes the meaning. Even so we know concerning our great Father:—

"He knows the thoughts we mean to speak,
Ere from our opening lips the break."

Do you therefore rejoice in this, that because the prayers of the Spirit are known and understood of God, therefore they will be sure to speed.

    The next argument for making us sure that they will speed is this—that they are "the mind of the Spirit." God the ever blessed is one, and there can be no division between the Father, the Son, and the Holy Ghost. These divine persons always work together, and there is a common desire for the glory of each blessed Person of the Divine Unity, and therefore it cannot be conceived without profanity, that anything could be the mind of the Holy Spirit and not be the mind of the Father and the mind of the Son. The mind of God is one and harmonious; if, therefore, the Holy Spirit dwells in you, and he move you to any desire, then his mind is in your prayer, and it is not possible that the eternal Father should reject your petitions. That prayer which came from heaven will certainly go back to heaven. If the Holy Ghost prompts it, the Father must and will accept it, for it is not possible that he should put a slight upon the ever blessed and adorable Spirit.

    But one more word, and that circles the argument, namely, that the work of the Spirit in the heart is not only the mind of the Spirit which God knows, but it is also according to the will or mind of God, for he never maketh intercession in us other than is consistent with the divine will. Now, the divine will or mind may be viewed two ways. First, there is the will declared in the proclamations of holiness by the Ten Commandments. The Spirit of God never prompts us to ask for anything that is unholy or inconsistent with the precepts of the Lord. Then secondly, there is the secret mind of God, the will of his eternal predestination and decree, of which we know nothing; but we do know this, that the Spirit of God never prompts us to ask anything which is contrary to the eternal purpose of God. Reflect for a moment: the Holy Spirit knows all the purposes of God, and when they are about to be fulfilled, he moves the children of God to pray about them, and so their prayers keep touch and tally with the divine decrees. Oh would you not pray confidently if you knew that your prayer corresponded with the sealed book of destiny? We may safely entreat the Lord to do what he has ordained to do. A carnal man draws the inference that if God has ordained an event we need not pray about it, but faith obediently draws the inference that the God who secretly ordained to give the blessing has openly commanded that we should pray for it, and therefore faith obediently prays. Coming events cast their shadows before them, and when God is about to bless his people his coming favour casts the shadow of prayer over the church. When he is about to favour an individual he casts the shadow of hopeful expectation over his soul. Our prayers, let men laugh at them as they will, and say there is no power in them, are the indicators of the movement of the wheels of Providence. Believing supplications are forecasts of the future, He who prayeth in faith is like the seer of old, he sees that which is to be: his holy expectancy, like a telescope, brings distant objects near to him. He is bold to declare that he has the petition which he has asked of God, and he therefore begins to rejoice and to praise God, even before the blessing has actually arrived. So it is: prayer prompted by the Holy Spirit is the footfall of the divine decree.

I conclude by saying, see, my dear hearers, the absolute necessity of the Holy Spirit, for if the saints know not what they should pray for as they ought; if consecrated men and women, with Christ suffering in them, still feel their need of the instruction of the Holy Spirit, how much more do you who are not saints, and have never given yourselves up to God, require divine teaching! On, that you would know and feel your dependence upon the Holy Ghost that he may prompt the once crucified but now ascended Redeemer that this gift of the Spirit, this promise of the Father, is shed abroad upon men. May he who comes from Jesus lead you to Jesus.

And, then O ye people of God, let this last thought abide with you,—what condescension is this that Divine Person should dwell in you for ever, and that he should be with you to help your prayers. Listen to me for a moment. If I read in the Scriptures that in the most heroic acts of faith God the Holy Ghost helpeth his people, I can understand it; if I read that in the sweetest music of their songs when they worship best, and chant their loftiest strains before the Most High God, the Spirit helpeth them, I can understand it; and even if I hear that in their wrestling prayers and prevalent intercessions God the Holy Spirit helpeth them, I can understand it: but I bow with reverent amazement, my heart sinking into the dust with adoration, when I reflect that God the Holy Ghost helps us when we cannot speak, but only groan. Yea, and when we cannot even utter our groanings, he doth not only help us but he claims as his own particular creation the "groanings that cannot be uttered." This is condescension indeed! In deigning to help us in the grief that cannot even vent itself in groaning, he proves himself to be a true Comforter. O God, my God, thou hast not forsaken me: thou art not far from me, nor from the voice of my roaring. Thou didst for awhile leave the Firstborn when he was made a curse for us, so that he cried in agony, "Why hast thou forsaken me?" but thou wilt not leave one of the "many brethren" for whom he died: the Spirit shall be with them, and when they cannot so much as groan he will make intercession for them with groanings that cannot be uttered. God bless you, my beloved brethren, and may you feel the Spirit of the Lord thus working in you and with you. Amen and amen.

Chapter 7
ADOPTION—THE SPIRIT AND THE CRY

"And because ye are sons, God hath sent forth the Spirit of his Son into your hearts, crying, Abba, Father."—Galatians 4:6.

We do not find the doctrine of the Trinity in Unity set forth in Scripture in formal terms, such as those which are employed in the Athanasian creed; but the truth is continually taken for granted, as if it were a fact well known in the church of God. If not laid down very often, in so many words, it is everywhere held in solution, and it is mentioned incidentally, in connection with other truths in a way which renders it quite as distinct as if it were expressed in a set formula. In many passages it is brought before us so prominently that we must be wilfully blind if we do not note it. In the present chapter, for instance, we have distinct mention of each of the three divine Persons. "God," that is the Father, "sent forth the Spirit," that is the Holy Spirit; and he is here called "the Spirit of his Son." Nor have we the names alone, for each sacred person is mentioned as acting in the work of our salvation: see the fourth verse, "God sent forth his Son."; then note the fifth verse, which speaks of the Son as redeeming them that were under the law; and then the text itself reveals the Spirit as coming into the hearts of believers, and crying Abba, Father. Now, inasmuch, as you have not only the mention of the separate names, but also certain special operations ascribed to each, it is plain that you have here the distinct personality of each. Neither the Father, the Son, nor the Spirit can be an influence, or a mere form of existence, for each one acts in a divine manner, but with a special sphere and a distinct mode of operation. The error of regarding a certain divine person as a mere influence, or emanation, mainly assails the Holy Ghost; but its falseness is seen in the words—"crying, Abba, Father": an influence could not cry; the act requires a person to perform it. Though we may not understand the wonderful truth of the undivided Unity, and the distinct personality of the Triune Godhead, yet, nevertheless, we see the truth revealed in the Holy Scriptures: and, therefore, we accept it as a matter of faith.

The divinity of each of these sacred persons is also to be gathered from the text and its connection. We do not doubt tee the loving union of all in the work of deliverance. We reverence the Father, without whom we had not been chosen or adopted: the Father who hath begotten us again unto a lively hope by the resurrection of Jesus Christ from the dead. We love and reverence the Son by whose most precious blood we have been redeemed, and with whom we are one in a mystic and everlasting union: and we adore and love the divine Spirit, for it is by him that we have been regenerated, illuminated, quickened, preserved, and sanctified; and it is through him that we receive the seal and witness within our hearts by which we are assured that we are indeed the sons of God. As God said of old, "Let us make man in our image, after our likeness, even so do the divine Persons take counsel together, and all unite in the new creation of the believer. We must not fail to bless, adore, and love each one of the exalted Persons, but we must diligently bow in lowliest reverence before the one God—Father, Son, and Holy Ghost. "Glory be to the Father, and to the Son, and to the Holy Ghost; as it was in the beginning, is now, and ever shall be, world without end. Amen."

Having noted this most important fact, let us come to the text itself, hoping to enjoy the doctrine of the Trinity while we are discoursing upon our adoption, in which wonder of grace they each have a share. Under the teaching of the divine Spirit may we be drawn into sweet communion with the Father through his Son Jesus Christ, to his glory and to our benefit.

Three things are very clearly set forth in my text: the first is the dignity of believers—"ye are sons;" the second is the consequent indwelling of the Holy Ghost—"because ye are sons, God hath sent forth the Spirit of his Son into your hearts;" and the third is the filial cry—crying, "Abba, Father."

I. First, then, THE DIGNITY OF BELIEVERS. Adoption gives us the rights of children, regeneration gives us the nature of children: we are partakers of both of these, for we are sons.

And let us here observe that this sonship is a gift of grace received by faith. We are not the sons of God by nature in the sense here meant. We are in a sense "the offspring God" by nature, but this is very different from the sonship here described, which is the peculiar privilege of those who are born again. The Jews claimed to be of the family of God, but as their privileges came to them by the way of their fleshly birth, they are likened to Ishmael, who was born after the flesh, but who was cast out as the son of the bondwoman, and compelled to give way to the son of the promise. We have a sonship which does not come to us by nature, for we are "born, not of blood, nor of the will of the flesh, nor of the will of man, but of God." Our sonship comes by promise, by the operation of God as a special gift to a peculiar seed, set apart unto the Lord by his own sovereign grace, as Isaac was. This honour and privilege come to us, according to the connection of our text, by faith. Note well the twenty-sixth verse of the preceding chapter (Gal. 3:26): "For ye are all the children of God by faith in Christ Jesus." As unbelievers we know nothing of adoption. While we are under the law as self-righteous we know something of servitude, but we know nothing of sonship. It is only after that faith has come that we cease to be under the schoolmaster, and rise out of our minority to take the privileges of the sons of God.

Faith worketh in us the spirit of adoption, and our consciousness of sonship, in this wise: first, it brings us justification. Verse twenty-four of the previous chapter says, "The law was our schoolmaster to bring us unto Christ, that we might be justified by faith." An unjustified man stands in the condition of a criminal, not of a child: his sin is laid to his charge, he is reckoned as unjust and unrighteous, as indeed he really is, and he is therefore a rebel against his king, and not a child enjoying his father's love. But when faith realizes the cleansing power of the blood of atonement, and lays hold upon the righteousness of God in Christ Jesus, then the justified man becomes a son and a child. Justification and adoption always go together. "Whom he called them he also justified," and the calling is a call to the Father's house, and to a recognition of sonship. Believing brings forgiveness and justification through our Lord Jesus; it also brings adoption, for it is written, "But as many as received him, to them gave he power to become the sons of God, even to them that believe on his name."

Faith brings us into the realization of our adoption in the next place by setting us free from the bondage of the law. "After that faith is come, we are no longer under a schoolmaster." When we groaned under a sense of sin, and were shut up by it as in a prison, we feared that the law would punish us for our iniquity, and our life was made bitter with fear. Moreover, we strove in our own blind self-sufficient manner to keep that law, and this brought us into yet another bondage, which became harder and harder as failure succeeded to failure: we sinned and stumbled more and more to our soul's confusion. But now that faith has come we see the law fulfilled in Christ, and ourselves justified and accepted in him: this changes the slave into a child, and duty into choice. Now we delight in the law, and by the power of the Spirit we walk in holiness to the glory of God. Thus it is that by believing in Christ Jesus we escape from Moses, the taskmaster, and come to Jesus, the Saviour; we cease to regard God as an angry Judge and view him as our loving Father. The system of merit and command, and punishment and fear, has given way to the rule of grace, gratitude, and love, and this new principle of government is one of the grand privileges of the children of God.

Now, faith is the mark of sonship in all who have it, whoever they may be, for "ye are all the children of God by faith in Christ Jesus Gal. 3:26). If you are believing in Jesus, whether you are Jew or Gentile, bond or free, you are a son of God. If you have only believed in Christ of late, and have but for the past few weeks been able to rest in his great salvation, yet, beloved, now are you a child of God. It is not an after privilege, granted to assurance or growth in grace; it is an early blessing, and belongs to him who has the smallest degree of faith, and is no more than a babe in grace. If a man be a believer in Jesus Christ his name is in the register-book of the great family above, "for ye are all the children of God by faith in Christ Jesus." But if you have no faith, no matter what zeal, no matter what works, no matter what knowledge, no matter what pretensions to holiness you may possess, you are nothing, and your religion is vain. Without faith in Christ you are as sounding brass and a tinkling cymbal, for without faith it is impossible to please God. Faith then, wherever it is found, is the infallible token of a child of God, and its absence is fatal to the claim.

This according to the apostle is further illustrated by our baptism, for in baptism, if there be faith in the soul, there is an open putting on of the Lord Jesus Christ. Read the twenty-seventh verse: "For as many of you as have been baptised into Christ have put on Christ." In baptism you professed to be dead to the world and you were therefore buried into the name of Jesus: and the meaning of that burial, if it had any right meaning to you, was that you professed yourself henceforth to be dead to everything but Christ, and henceforth your life was to be in him, and you were to be as one raised from the dead to newness of life. Of course the outward form avails nothing to the unbeliever, but to the man who is in Christ it is a most instructive ordinance. The spirit and essence of the ordinance lie in the soul's entering into the symbol, in the man's knowing not alone the baptism into water, but the baptism into the Holy Ghost and into fire: and as many of you as know that inward mystic baptism into Christ know also that henceforth you have put on Christ and are covered by him as a man is by his garment. Henceforth you are one in Christ, you wear his name, you live in him, you are saved by him, you are altogether his. Now, if you are one with Christ, since he is a son, you are sons also. If you have put on Christ God seeth you not in yourself but in Christ, and that which belongeth unto Christ belongeth also unto you, for if you be Christ's then are you Abraham's seed and heirs according to the promise. As the Roman youth when he came of age put on the toga, and was admitted to the rights of citizenship, so the putting on of Christ is the token of our admission into the position of sons of God. Thus are we actually admitted to the enjoyment of our glorious heritage. Every blessing of the covenant of grace belongs to those who are Christ's, and every believer is in that list. Thus, then, according to the teaching of the passage, we receive adoption by faith as the gift of grace.

Again, adoption comes to us by redemption. Read the passage which precedes the text: "But when the fullness of the time was come, God sent forth his Son, made of a woman, made under the law, to redeem them that were under the law, that we might receive the adoption of sons." Beloved, prize redemption, and never listen to teaching which would destroy its meaning or lower its importance. Remember that ye were not redeemed with silver and gold, but with the precious blood of Christ, as of a lamb without blemish. You were under the law, and subject to its curse, for you had broken it most grievously, and you were subject to its penalty, for it is written, "the soul that sinneth, it shall die"; and yet again, "cursed is everyone that continueth not in all things that are written in the book of the law to do them." You were also under the terror of the law, for you feared its wrath; and you were under its irritating power, for often when the commandment came, sin within you revived and you died. But now you are redeemed from all; as the Holy Ghost saith, "Christ hath redeemed us from the curse of the law, being made a curse for us: for it is written, Cursed is every one that hangeth on a tree." Now ye are not under the law, but under grace, and this because Christ came under the law and kept it both by his active and his passive obedience, fulfilling all its commands and bearing all its penalty on your behalf and in your room and stead. Henceforth you are the redeemed of the Lord, and enjoy a liberty which comes by no other way but that of the eternal ransom. Remember this; and whenever you feel most assured that you are a child of God, praise the redeeming blood; whenever your heart beats highest with love to your great Father, bless the "firstborn among many brethren," who for your sakes came under the law, was circumcised, kept the law in his life, and bowed his head to it in his death, honouring, and magnifying the law, and making the justice and righteousness of God to be more conspicuous by his life than it would have been by the holiness of all mankind, and his justice to be more fully vindicated by his death that it would have been if all the world of sinners had been cast into hell. Glory be to our redeeming Lord, by whom we have received the adoption!

Again, we further learn from the passage that we now enjoy the privilege of sonship. According to the run of the passage the apostle means not only that we are children, but that we are full-grown sons. "Because ye are sons," means,—because the time appointed of the Father is come, and you are of age, and no longer under tutors and governors. In our minority we are under the schoolmaster, under the regimen of ceremonies, under types, figures, shadows, learning our A B C by being convinced of sin; but when faith is come we are no longer under the schoolmaster, but come to a more free condition. Till faith comes we are under tutors and governors, like mere boys, but after faith we take our rights as sons of God. The Jewish church of old was under the yoke of the law; its sacrifices were continual and its ceremonies endless; new moons and feasts must be kept; jubilees must be observed and pilgrimages made: in fact, the yoke was too heavy for feeble flesh to bear. The law followed the Israelite into every corner, and dealt with him upon every point: it had to do with his garments, his meat, his drink, his bed, his board, and everything about him: it treated him like a boy at school who has a rule for everything. Now that faith has come we are full grown sons, and therefore we are free from the rules which govern the school of the child. We are under law to Christ, even as the full-grown son is still under the discipline of his father's house; but this is a law of love and not of fear, of grace and not of bondage. "Stand fast therefore in the liberty wherewith Christ hath made us free, and be not entangled again with the yoke of bondage." Return not to the beggarly elements of a merely outward religion, but keep close to the worship of God in spirit and in truth, for this is the liberty of the children of God.

Now, by faith we are no more like to bond-servants. The apostle says that "the heir, as long as he is a child, differeth nothing from a servant, though he be lord of all; but is under tutor and governors till the time appointed of the father." But beloved, now are ye the sons of God, and ye have come to your majority: now are ye free to enjoy the honours and blessings of the Father's house. Rejoice that the free spirit dwells within you, and prompts you to holiness; this is a far superior power to the merely external command and the whip of threatening. Now no more are you in bondage to outward forms, and rites, and ceremonies; but the Spirit of God teacheth you all things, and leads you into the inner meaning and substance of the truth.

Now, also, saith the apostle, we are heirs—"Wherefore thou art no more a servant, but a son; and if a son, then an heir of God through Christ." No man living has ever realised to the full what this means. Believers are at this moment heirs, but what is the estate? It is God himself! We are heirs of God! Not only of the promises, of the covenant engagements, and of all the blessings which belong to the chosen seed, but heirs of God himself. "The Lord is my portion, saith my soul." "This God is our God for ever and ever." We are not only, heirs to God, to all that he gives to his firstborn, but heirs of God himself. David said, "The Lord is the portion of mine inheritance and of my cup." As he said to Abraham, "Fear not Abraham, I am thy shield and thine exceeding great reward," so saith he to every man that is born of the Spirit. These are his own words—"I will be to them a God, and they shall be to me a people." Why, then, O believer, are you poor? All riches are yours. Why then are you sorrowful? The ever-blessed God is yours. Why do you tremble? Omnipotence waits to help you. Why do you distrust? His immutability will abide with you even to the end, and make his promise steadfast. All things are yours, for Christ is yours, and Christ is God's; and though there be some things which at present you cannot actually grasp in your hand, nor even see with your eye, to wit, the things which are laid up for you in heaven, yet still by faith you can enjoy even these, for "he hath raised us up together, and made us sit together in the heavenlies in Christ," "in whom also we have obtained an inheritance," so that "our citizenship is in heaven." We enjoy even now the pledge and earnest of heaven in the indwelling of the Holy Ghost. Oh what privileges belong to those who are the sons of God!

Once more upon this point of the believer's dignity, we are already tasting one of the inevitable consequences of being the sons of God. What are they? One of them is the opposition of the children of the bondwoman. No sooner had the apostle Paul preached the liberty of the saints, than straightway there arose certain teachers who said, "This will never do; you must be circumcised, you must come under the law." Their opposition was to Paul a token that he was of the free woman, for behold the children of the bondwoman singled him out for their virulent opposition. You shall find, dear brother, that if you enjoy fellowship with God, if you live in the spirit of adoption, if you are brought near to the Most High, so as to be a member of the divine family, straightway all those who are under bondage to the law will quarrel with you. Thus saith the apostle, "As then he that was born after the flesh persecuted him that was born after the Spirit, even so it is now." The child of Hagar was found by Sarah mocking Isaac, the child of promise. Ishmael would have been glad to have shown his enmity to the hated heir by blows and personal assault, but there was a superior power to check him, so that he could get no further than "mocking." So it is just now. There have been periods in which the enemies of the gospel have gone a great deal further than mocking, for they have been able to imprison and burn alive the lovers of the gospel; but now, thank God, we are under his special protection as to life and limb and liberty, and are as safe as Isaac was in Abraham's house. They can mock us, but they cannot go any further, or else some of us would be publicly gibbeted. But trials of cruel mockings are still to be endured, our words are twisted, our sentiments are misrepresented, and all sorts of horrible things are imputed to us, things which we know not, to all which we would reply with Paul, "Am I therefore become your enemy because I tell you the truth?" This is the old way of the Hagarenes, the child after the flesh is still doing his best to mock him that is born after the Spirit. Do not be astonished, neither be grieved in the least degree when this happens to any of you, but let this also turn to the establishment of your confidence and to the confirmation of your faith in Christ Jesus, for he told you of old, "If ye were of the world, the world would love his own: but because ye are not of the world, but I have chosen you out of the world, therefore the world hateth you."

II. Our second head is THE CONSEQUENT INDWELLING OF THE HOLY GHOST IN BELIEVERS;—"God hath sent forth the Spirit of his Son into your hearts." Here is a divine act of the Father. The Holy Ghost proceedeth from the Father and the Son: and God hath sent him forth into your hearts. If he had only come knocking at your hearts and asked your leave to enter, he had never entered, but when Jehovah sent him he made his way, without violating your will, but yet with irresistible power. Where Jehovah sent him there he will abide, and go no more out for ever. Beloved, I have no time to dwell upon the words, but I want you to turn them over in your thoughts, for they contain a great depth. As surely as God sent his Son into the world to dwell among men, so that his saints beheld his glory, the "glory as of the only begotten of the Father, full of grace and truth," so surely hath God sent forth the Spirit to enter into men's hearts, there to take up his residence that in him also the glory of God may be revealed. Bless and adore the Lord who hath sent you such a visitor as this.

Now, note the style and title under which the Holy Spirit comes to us: he comes as the Spirit of Jesus. The words are "the Spirit of his Son," by which is not meant the character and disposition of Christ, though that were quite true, for God sends this unto his people, but it means the Holy Ghost. Why, then, is he called the Spirit of his Son, or the Spirit of Jesus? May we not give these reasons? It was by the Holy Ghost that the human nature of Christ was born of the Virgin. By the Spirit our Lord was attested at his baptism, when the Holy Spirit descended upon him like a dove, and abode upon him. In him the Holy Spirit dwelt without measure, anointing him for his great work, and by the Spirit he was anointed with the oil of gladness above his fellows. The Spirit was also with him, attesting his ministry by signs and wonders. The Holy Ghost is our Lord's great gift to the church; it was after his ascension that he bestowed the gifts of Pentecost, and the Holy Spirit descended upon the church to abide with the people of God for ever. The Holy Ghost is the Spirit of Christ, because, also, he is Christ's witness here below; for "there are three that bear witness on earth, the Spirit, and the water, and the blood." For these and many other reasons he is called "the Spirit of his Son," and it is he who comes to dwell in believers. I would urge you very solemnly and gratefully to consider the wondrous condescension which is here displayed. God himself the Holy Ghost, takes up his residence in believers. I never know which is the more wonderful, the incarnation of Christ or the indwelling of the Holy Ghost. Jesus dwelt here for awhile in human flesh untainted by sin, holy, harmless, undefiled, and separate from sinners; but the Holy Ghost dwells continually in the hearts of all believers, though as yet they are imperfect and prone to evil. Year after year, century after century, he still abideth in the saints, and will do so till the elect are all in glory. While we adore the incarnate Son, let us adore also the indwelling Spirit whom the Father hath sent.

Now notice the place wherein he takes up his residence.—"God hath sent forth the Spirit of his Son into your hearts." Note, that it does not say into your heads or your brains. The Spirit of God doubtless illuminates the intellect and guides the judgement, but this is not the commencement nor the main part of his work. He comes chiefly to the affections, he dwells with the heart, for with the heart man believeth unto righteousness, and "God hath sent forth the Spirit of his Son into your hearts." Now, the heart is the centre of our being, and therefore doth the Holy Ghost occupy this place of vantage. He comes into the central fortress and universal citadel of our nature, and thus takes possession of the whole. The heart is the vital part; we speak of it as the chief residence of life, and therefore the Holy Ghost enters it, and as the living God dwells in the living heart, taking possession of the very core and marrow of our being. It is from the heart and through the heart that life is diffused. The blood is sent even to the extremities of the body by the pulsings of the heart, and when the Spirit of God takes possession of the affections, he operates upon every power, and faculty, and member of our entire manhood. Out of the heart are the issues of life, and from the affections sanctified by the Holy Ghost all other faculties and powers receive renewal, illumination, sanctification, strengthening, and ultimate perfection.

This wonderful blessing is ours "because we are sons;" and it is fraught with marvellous results. Sonship sealed by the indwelling Spirit brings us peace and joy; it leads to nearness to God and fellowship with him; it excites trust, love, and vehement desire, and creates in us reverence, obedience, and actual likeness to God. All this, and much more, because the Holy Ghost has come to dwell in us. Oh, matchless mystery! Had it not been revealed it had never been imagined, and now that it is revealed it would never have been believed if it had not become matter of actual experience to those who are in Christ Jesus. There are many professors who know nothing of this; they listen to us with bewilderment as if we told them an idle tale, for the carnal mind knoweth not the things that be of God; they are spiritual, and can only be spiritually discerned. Those who are not sons, or who only come in as sons under the law of nature, like Ishmael, know nothing of this indwelling Spirit, and are up in arms at us for daring to claim so great a blessing: yet it is ours, and none can deprive us of it.

III. Now I come to the third portion of our text—THE FILIAL CRY. This is deeply interesting. I think it will be profitable if your minds enter into it. Where the Holy Ghost enters there is a cry. "God hath sent forth the Spirit of his Son, crying, 'Abba, Father.'" Now, notice, it is the Spirit of God that cries —a most remarkable fact. Some are inclined to view the expression as a

Hebraism, and read it, he "makes us to cry;" but, beloved, the text saith not so, and we are not at liberty to alter it upon such a pretence. We are always right in keeping to what God says, and here we plainly read of the Spirit in our hearts that he is crying "Abba, Father." The apostle in Romans 8:15 says, "Ye have received the Spirit of adoption, whereby we cry, Abba, Father," but here he describes the Spirit himself as crying "Abba, Father." We are certain that when he ascribed the cry of "Abba, Father" to us, he did not wish to exclude the Spirit's cry, because in the twenty-sixth verse of the famous eighth of Romans he says, "Likewise the Spirit also helpeth our infirmities: for we know not what we should pray for as we ought: but the Spirit itself maketh intercession for us with groanings which cannot be uttered." Thus he represents the Spirit himself as groaning with unutterable groanings within the child of God, so that when he wrote to the Romans he had on his mind the same thought which he here expressed to the Galatians,—that it is the Spirit itself which cries and groans in us "Abba, Father." How is this? Is it not ourselves that cry? Yes, assuredly; and yet the Spirit cries also. The expressions are both correct. The Holy Spirit prompts and inspires the cry. He puts the cry into the heart and mouth of the believer. It is his cry because he suggests it, approves of it, and educates us to it. We should never have cried thus if he had not first taught us the way. As a mother teaches her child to speak, so he puts this cry of "Abba, Father" into our mouths; yea, it is he who forms in our hearts the desire after our Father, God, and keeps it there. He is the Spirit of adoption, and the author of adoption's special and significant cry.

Not only does he prompt us to cry but he works in us a sense of need which compels us to cry, and also that spirit of confidence which emboldens us to claim such relationship to the great God. Nor is this all, for he assists us in some mysterious manner so that we are able to pray aright; he puts his divine energy into us so that we cry "Abba, Father" in an acceptable manner. There are times when we cannot cry at all, and then he cries in us. There are seasons when doubts and fears abound, and so suffocate us with their fumes that we cannot even raise a cry, and then the indwelling Spirit represents us, and speaks for us, and makes intercession for us, crying in our name, and making intercession for us according to the will of God. Thus does the cry "Abba, Father" rise up in our hearts even when we feel as if we could not pray and dare not think ourselves children. Then we may each say, "I live, yet not I, but the Spirit that dwelleth in me." On the other hand, at times our soul gives such a sweet assent to the Spirit's cry that it becometh ours also, but then we more than ever own the work of the Spirit, and still ascribe to him the blessed cry, "Abba, Father."

I want you now to notice a very sweet fact about this cry; namely, that it is literally the cry of the Son. God hath sent the Spirit of his Son into our hearts, and that Spirit cries in us exactly according to the cry of the Son. If you turn to the gospel of Mark, at the fourteenth chapter, thirty-sixth verse, you will find there what you will not discover in any other evangelist (for Mark is always the man for the striking points, and the memorable words), he records that our Lord prayed in the garden, "Abba, Father, all things are possible unto thee; take away this cup from me: nevertheless not what I will, but what thou wilt." So that this cry in us copies the cry of our Lord to the letter—"Abba, Father." Now, I dare say you have heard these words "Abba, Father" explained at considerable lengths at other times, and if so, you know that the first word is Syrian or Aramaic; or, roughly speaking, Abba is the Hebrew word for "father." The second word is in Greek, and is the Gentile word, "pates," or pater, which also signifies father. It is said that these two words are used to remind us that Jews and Gentiles are one before God. They do remind us of this, but this cannot have been the principal reason for their use. Do you think that when our Lord was in his agony in the garden that he said, "Abba, Father" because Jews and Gentiles are one? Why should he have thought of that doctrine, and why need he mention it in prayer to his Father? Some other reason must have suggested it to him. It seems to me that our Lord said "Abba" because it was his native tongue. When a Frenchman prays, if he has learned English he may ordinarily pray in English, but if ever he falls into an agony he will pray in French, as surely as he prays at all. Our Welsh brethren tell us that there is no language like Welsh—I suppose it is so to them: now they will talk English when about their ordinary business, and they can pray in English when everything goes comfortably with them, but I am sure that if a Welshman is in a great fervency of prayer, he flies to his Welsh tongue to find full expression. Our Lord in his agony used his native language, and as born of the seed of Abraham he cries in his own tongue, Abba. Even thus, my brethren, we are prompted by the spirit of adoption to use our own language, the language of the heart, and to speak to the Lord freely in our own tongue. Besides, to my mind, the word "Abba" is of all words in all languages the most natural word for father. I must try and pronounce it so that you see the natural childishness of it, "Ab—ba," "Ab—

ba." Is it not just what your children say, ab, ab, ba, ba, as soon as they try to talk? It is the sort of word which any child would say, whether Hebrew, or Greek, or French, or English. Therefore, Abba is a word worthy of introduction into all languages. It is truly a child's word, and our Master felt, I have no doubt, in his agony, a love for child's words. Dr. Guthrie, when he was dying, said, "Sing a hymn," but he added, "Sing me one of the bairns' hymns." When a man comes to die he wants to be a child again, and longs for bairns' hymns and bairns' words. Our blessed Master in his agony used the bairns' word, "Abba," and it is equally becoming in the mouth of each one of us. I think this sweet word "Abba" was chosen to show us that we are to be very natural with God, and not stilted and formal. We are to be very affectionate, and come close to him, and not merely say "Pater," which is a cold Greek word, but say "Abba," which is a warm, natural, loving word, fit for one who is a little child with God, and makes bold to lie in his bosom, and look up into his face and talk with holy boldness. "Abba" is not a word, somehow, but a babe's lisping. Oh, how near we are to God when we can use such a speech! How dear he is to us and dear we are to him when we may thus address him, saying, like the great Son himself, "Abba, Father."

This leads me to observe that this cry in our hearts is exceedingly near and familiar. In the sound of it I have shown you that it is childlike, but the tone and manner of the utterance are equally so. Note that it is a cry. If we obtain audience with a king we do not cry, we speak then in measured tones and set phrases; but the Spirit of God breaks down our measured tones, and takes away the formality which some hold in great admiration, and he leads us to cry, which is the very reverse of formality and stiffness. When we cry, we cry, "Abba": even our very cries are full of the spirit of adoption. A cry is a sound which we are not anxious that every passer-by should hear; yet what child minds his father hearing him cry? So when our heart is broken and subdued we do not feel as if we could talk fine language at all, but the Spirit in us sends forth cries and groans, and of these we are not ashamed, nor are we afraid to cry before God. I know some of you think that God will not hear your prayers, because you cannot pray grandly like such-and-such a minister. Oh, but the Spirit of his Son cries, and you cannot do better than cry too. Be satisfied to offer to God broken language, words salted with your griefs, wetted with your tears. Go to him with holy familiarity, and be not afraid to cry in his presence, "Abba, Father."

But then how earnest it is: for a cry is an intense thing. The word implies fervency. A cry is not a flippant utterance, nor a mere thing of the lips, it comes up from the soul. Hath not the Lord taught us to cry to him in prayer with fervent importunity that will not take a denial? Hath he not brought us so near to him that sometimes we say, "I will not let thee go except thou bless me"? Hath he not taught us so to pray that his disciples might almost say of us as they did of one of old, "Send her away, for she crieth after us." We do cry after him, our heart and our flesh crieth out for God, for the living God, and this is the cry, "Abba, Father, I must know thee, I must taste thy love, I must dwell under thy wing, I must behold thy face, I must feel thy great fatherly heart overflowing and filling my heart with peace." We cry, "Abba, Father."

   I shall close when I notice this, that the most of this crying is kept within the heart, and does not come out at the lips. Like Moses, we cry when we say not a word. God hath sent forth the Spirit of his Son into our hearts, whereby we cry, "Abba, Father." You know what I mean: it is not alone in your little room, by the old arm-chair, that you cry to God, but you call him "Abba, Father," as you go about the streets or work in the shop. The Spirit of his Son is crying "Abba, Father," when you are in the crowd or at your table among the family. I see it is alleged as a very grave charge against me that I speak as if I were familiar with God. If it be so, I make bold to say that I speak only as I feel. Blessed be my heavenly Father's name, I know I am his child, and with whom should a child be familiar but with his father? O ye strangers to the living God, be it known unto you that if this be vile, I purpose to be viler still, as he shall help me to walk more closely with him. We feel a deep reverence for our Father in heaven, which bows us to the very dust, but for all that we can say, "truly our fellowship is with the Father and with his Son, Jesus Christ." No stranger can understand the nearness of the believer's soul to God in Christ Jesus, and because the world cannot understand it, it finds it convenient to sneer, but what of that? Abraham's tenderness to Isaac made Ishmael jealous, and caused him to laugh, but Isaac had no cause to be ashamed of being ridiculed, since the mocker could not rob him of the covenant blessing. Yes, beloved, the Spirit of God makes you cry "Abba, Father," but the cry is mainly within your heart, and there it is so commonly uttered that it becomes the habit of your soul to be crying to your Heavenly Father. The text does not say that he had cried, but the expression is "crying"—it is a present participle, indicating that he cries every day "Abba, Father." Go home, my brethren, and live in the spirit of sonship. Wake up in the morning, and let your first thought be "My Father, my Father, be with me this day. Go out into business, and when things perplex you let that be your resort—"My Father, help me in this hour of need." When you go to your home, and there meet with domestic anxieties, let your cry sill be, "Help me, my Father." When alone you are not alone, because the Father is with you: and in the midst of the crowd you are not in danger, because the Father himself loveth you. What a blessed word is that,—"The Father himself loveth you"! Go, and live as his children. Take heed that ye reverence him, for if he be a father where is his fear? Go and obey him, for this is right. Be ye imitators of God as dear children. Honour him wherever you are, by adorning his doctrine in all things. Go and live upon him, for you shall soon live with him. Go and rejoice in him. Go and cast all your cares upon him. Go henceforth, and whatever men may see in you may they be compelled to own that you are the children of the Highest. "Blessed are the peacemakers, for they shall be called the children of God." May you be such henceforth and evermore. Amen and amen.

Chapter 8
GRIEVING THE HOLY SPIRIT

"And grieve not the Holy Spirit of God, whereby ye are sealed unto the day of redemption."—Ephesians 4:30.

There is something very touching in this admonition, "Grieve not the Holy Spirit of God." It does not say, "Do not make him angry." A more delicate and tender term is used—"Grieve him not." There are some men of so hard a character, that to make another angry does not give them much pain; and indeed, there are many of us who are scarcely to be moved by the information that another is angry with us; but where is the heart so hard, that it is not moved when we know that we have caused others grief?—for grief is a sweet combination of anger and of love. It is anger, but all the gall is taken from it. Love sweetens the anger, and turns the edge of it, not against the person, but against the offense. We all know how we use the two terms in contra-distinction the one to the other. When I commit any offense, some friend who hath but little patience, suddenly snaps asunder his forbearance and is angry with me. The same offense is observed by a loving father, and he is grieved. There is anger in his bosom, but he is angry and he sins not, for he is angry against my sin; and yet there is love to neutralize and modify the anger towards me. Instead of wishing me ill as the punishment of my sin, he looks upon my sin itself as being the ill. He grieves to think that I am already injured, from the fact that I have sinned. I say this is a heavenly compound, more precious than all the ointment of the merchants. There may be the bitterness of myrrh, but there is all the sweetness of frankincense in this sweet term "to grieve." I am certain, my hearers, I do not flatter you when I declare, that I am sure that the most of you would grieve, if you thought you were grieving anyone else. You, perhaps, would not care much if you had made any one angry without a cause; but to grieve him, even though it were without a cause and without intention, would nevertheless cause you distress of heart, and you would not rest until this grief had subsided, till you had made some explanation or apology, and had done your best to allay the smart and take away the grief. When we see anger in another, we at once begin to feel hostility. Anger begets anger; but grief begets pity, and pity is next akin to love; and we love those whom we have caused to grieve. Now, is not this a very sweet expression—"Grieve not the Holy Spirit?" Of course, the language is be to understood as speaking after the manner of men. The Holy Spirit of God knoweth no passion or suffering, but nevertheless, his emotion is here described in human language as being that of grief. And is it not, I say a tender and touching thing, that the Holy Spirit should direct his servant Paul to say to us "Grieve not the Holy Spirit," do not excite his loving anger, do not vex him, do not cause him to mourn? He is a dove; do not cause him to mourn, because you have treated him harshly and ungratefully. Now, the purport of my sermon, this morning, will be to exhort you not to grieve the Spirit; but I shall divide it thus:—first, I shall discourse upon the love of the Spirit; secondly, upon the seal of the Spirit; and then, thirdly, upon the grieving of the Spirit.

I. The few words I have to say UPON THE LOVE OF THE SPIRIT will all be pressing forward to my great mark, stirring you up not to grieve the Spirit; for when we are persuaded that another loves us, we find at once a very potent reason why we should not grieve him. The love of the Spirit!—how shall I tell it forth? Surely it needs a songster to sing it, for love is only to be spoken of in words of song. The love of the Spirit!—let me tell you of his early love to us. He loved us without beginning. In the eternal covenant of grace, as I told you last Sabbath, he was one of the high contracting parties in the divine contract, whereby we are saved. All that can be said of the love of the Father, of the love of the Son, may be said of the love of the Spirit—it is eternal, it is infinite, it is sovereign, it is everlasting, it is a love which cannot be dissolved, which cannot be decreased, a love which cannot be removed from those who are the objects of it. Permit me, however, to refer you to his acts, rather than his attributes. Let me tell you of the love of the Spirit to you and to me. Oh how early was that love which he manifested towards us, even in our childhood! My brethren, we can well remember how the Spirit was wont to strive with us. We went astray from the womb speaking lies, but how early did the Spirit of God stir up our conscience, and solemnly correct us on account of our youthful sins. How frequently since then has the Spirit wooed us! How often under the ministry has he compelled our hearts to melt, and the tear has run down our cheeks, and he has sweetly whispered in our ear, "My son, give me thy heart; go to thy chamber, shut thy door about thee, confess thy sins, and seek a Saviour's love and blood." Oh,—but let us blush to tell it—how often have we done despite to him! When we were in a state of unregeneracy, how we were wont to resist him! We quenched the Spirit; he strove with us but we strove against him. But blessed be his dear name, and let him have everlasting songs for it, he would not let us go! We would not be saved, but he would save us. We sought to thrust ourselves into the fire, but he sought to pluck us from the burning. We would dash ourselves from the precipice, but he wrestled with us and held us fast; he would not let us destroy our souls. Oh, how we ill-treated him, how we did set at nought his counsel! How did we scorn and scoff him; how did we despise the ordinance which would lead us to Christ! How did we violate that holy cord which was gently drawing us to Jesus and his cross! I am sure, my brethen, at the recollections of the persevering struggles of the Spirit with you, you must be stirred up to love him. How often did he restrain you from sin, when you were about to plunge headlong into a course of vice! How often did he constrain you to good, when you would have neglected it! You, perhaps, would not have been in the way at all, and the Lord would not have met you, if it had not been for that sweet Spirit, who would not let you become a blasphemer, who would not suffer you to forsake the house of God, and would not permit you to become a regular attendant at the haunts of vice, but checked you, and held you in, as it were, with bit and bridle. Though you were like a bullock, unaccustomed to the yoke, yet he would not let you have your way. Though you struggled against him, yet he would not throw the reins upon your necks, but he said, "I will have him, I will have him against his will; I will change his heart, I will not let him go till I have made him a trophy of my mighty power to save." And then think my brethren of the love of the Spirit after that—

"Dost mind the time, the spot of land,
Where Jesus did thee meet?
Where he first took thee by the hand,
Thy bridegroom's love—how sweet!"

Ah, then, in that blest hour, to memory dear, was it not the Holy Spirit who guided you to Jesus? Do you remember the love of the Spirit, when, after having quickened you, he took you aside, and showed you Jesus on the tree? Who was it that opened our blind eye to see a dying Saviour? Who was it that opened your deaf ear to hear the voice of pardoning love? Who opened your clasped and palsied hand to receive the tokens of a Saviour's grace Who was it that brake your hard heart and made a way for the Saviour to enter and dwell therein? Oh! it was that precious Spirit that self-same Spirit, to whom you had done so much despite, whom in the days of your flesh you had resisted! What a mercy it was that he did not say, "I will swear in my wrath that they shall not enter into my rest, for they have vexed me, and I will take my everlasting flight from them;" or thus, "Ephraim is joined unto idols, I will let him alone!" And since that time, my brethren, how sweetly has the Spirit proved his love to you and to me. It is not only in his first strivings, and then his divine quickenings; but in all the sequel, how much have we owed to his instruction. We have been dull scholars with the word before us, plain and simple, so that he that reads may read, and he that reads may understand, yet how small a portion of his Word has our memory retained, how little progress have we made in the school of God's grace! We are but learners yet, unstable, weak, and apt to slide, but what a blessed instructor we have had! Has he not led us into many a truth, and taken of the things of Christ and applied them unto us? Oh! When I think how stupid I have been, I wonder that he has not given me up. When I think what a dolt I have been, when he would have taught me the things of the kingdom of God, I marvel that he should have had such patience with me. Is it a wonder that Jesus should become a babe? Is it not an equal wonder that the Spirit of the living God, should become a teacher of babes? It is a marvel that Jesus should lie in a manger; is it not an equal marvel that the Holy Spirit should become an usher in the sacred school, to teach fools, and make them wise? It was condescension that brought the Saviour to the cross, but is it not equal condescension that brings the mighty Spirit of grace down to dwell with stubborn unruly, wild asses' colts, to teach them the mystery of the kingdom, and make them know the wonders of a Saviour's love?

Furthermore, my brethren, forget not how much we owe to the Spirit's consolation, how much has he manifested his love to you in cherishing you in all your sicknesses, assisting you in all your labors; and comforting you in all your distresses. He has been a blessed comforter to me I can testify; when every other comfort failed, when the promise itself seemed empty, when the ministry was void of power, it is then the Holy Spirit has proved a rich comfort unto my soul, and filled my poor heart with peace and joy in believing. How many times would your heart have broken if the Spirit had not bound it up! How often has he who is your teacher become also your physician, has closed the wounds of your poor bleeding spirit, and has bound up those wounds with the court plaister of the promise, and so has stanched the bleeding, and has given you back your spiritual health once more. It does seem to rise a marvel that the Holy Ghost should become a comforter, for comforting is, to many minds, but an inferior work in the church, though really it is not so. To teach, to preach, to command with authority, how many are willing to do this because this is honorable work; but to sit down and bear with the infirmities of the creature, to enter into all the stratagems of unbelief, to find the soul a way of peace in the midst of seas of trouble this is compassion like a God, that the Holy Spirit should stoop from heaven to become a comforter of disconsolate spirits. What! must he himself bring the cordial? must he wait upon his sick child and stand by his bed? must he make his bed for him in his afflictions must he carry him in his infirmity? must he breathe continually into him his very breath? Doth the Holy Spirit become a waiting servant of the church? Doth he become a lamp to enlighten? and doth he become a staff on which we may lean? This, I say, should move us to love the Holy Spirit, for we have in all this abundant proofs of his love to us.

Stay not here, beloved, there are larger fields yet beyond, now that we are speaking of the love of the Spirit. Remember how much he loves us when he helpeth our infirmities. Nay, not only doth he help our infirmities, but when we know not what to pray for as we ought he teacheth us how to pray, and when "we ourselves groan within ourselves," then the Spirit himself maketh intersession for us with groanings which cannot be uttered—groans as we should groan, but more audibly, so that our prayer, which else would have been silent, reaches the ears of Christ, and is then presented before his Father's face. To help our infirmities is a mighty instance of love. When God overcomes infirmity altogether, or removes it, there is something very noble, and grand, and sublime in the deed; when he permits the infirmity to remain and yet works with the infirmity, this is tender compassion indeed. When the Saviour heals the lame man you see his Godhead, but when he walketh with the lame man, limping though his gait may be; when he sitteth with the beggar, when he talketh with the publican, when he carryeth the babe in his bosom, then this helping of infirmities is a manifestation of love almost unequalled. Save Christ's bearing our infirmities upon the tree and our sins in his own body, I know of no greater or more tender instance of divine love than when it is written, "Likewise the Spirit also helpeth our infirmities." Oh how much you owe to the Spirit when you have been on your knees in prayer! You know, my brethren, what it is to be dull and lifeless there; to groan for a word, and yet you cannot find it; to wish for a word, and yet the very wish is languid; to long to have desires, and yet all the desire you have is a desire that you may be able to desire. Oh, have you not sometimes, when your desires have been kindled longed to get a grip at the promise by the hand of faith? "Oh," you have said, "if I could but plead the promise, all my necessities would be removed, and all my sorrows would be allayed;" but, alas, the promise was beyond your reach. If you touched it with the tip of your finger, you could not grasp it as you desired, you could not plead it, and therefore you came away without the blessing. But when the Spirit has helped our infirmities how have we prayed! Why, there have been times when you and I have so grasped the knocker of the gate of mercy, and have let it fall with such tremendous force, that it seemed as if the very gate itself did shake and totter; there have been seasons when we have laid hold upon the angel, have overcome heaven by prayer, have declared we would not let Jehovah himself go except he should bless us. We have, and we say it without blasphemy, moved the arm that moves the world. We have brought down upon us the eyes that look upon the universe. All this we have done, not by our own strength, but by the might and by the power of the Spirit, and seeing he has so sweetly enabled us, though we have so often forgotten to thank him; seeing that he has so graciously assisted us though we have often taken all the glory to ourselves instead of airing it to him, must we not admire his love, and must it not be a fearful sin indeed to grieve the Holy Spirit by whom we are sealed?

Another token of the Spirit's love remains, namely, his indwelling in the saints. We sing in one of our hymns,—
"Dost thou not dwell in all the saints?"

We ask a question which can have but one answer. He does dwell in the heart of all God's redeemed and blood-washed people. And what a condescension is this, that he whom the heaven of heavens cannot contain, dwells in thy breast my brother. That breast often covered with rags, may be a breast often agitated with anxious care and thought, a breast too often defiled with sin, and yet he dwells there. The little narrow heart of man the Holy Spirit hath made his palace. Though it is but a cottage, a very hovel, and all unholy and unclean yet doth the Holy Spirit condescend to make the heart of his people his continual abode. Oh my friends, when I think how often you and I have let the devil in, I wonder the Spirit has not withdrawn from us. The final perseverance of the saints, is one of the greatest miracles on record; in fact, it is the sum total of miracles. The perseverance of a saint for a single day, is a multitude of miracles of mercy. When you consider that the Spirit is of purer eyes than to behold iniquity, and yet he dwells in the heart where sin often intrudes, a heart out of which comes blasphemies, and murders, and all manner of evil thoughts and concupiscence, what if sometimes he is grieved, and retires and leaves us to ourselves for a season? It is a marvel that he is there at all, for he must be daily grieved with these evil guests, these false traitors, these base intruders who thrust themselves into that little temple which he has honored with his presence, the temple of the heart of man. I am afraid, dear friends, we are too much in the habit of talking of the love of Jesus, without thinking of the love of the Holy Spirit. Now I would not wish to exalt one person of the Trinity above another, but I do feel this, that because Jesus Christ was a man, bone of our bone, and flesh of our flesh, and therefore there was something tangible in him that can be seen with the eyes, and handled with the hands, therefore we more readily think of him, and fix our love on him, than we do upon the Spirit. But why should it be? Let us love Jesus with all our hearts, and let us love the Holy Spirit too. Let us have songs for him, gratitude for him. We do not forget Christ's cross, let us not forget the Spirit's operations. We do not forget what Jesus has done for us, let us always remember what the Spirit does in us. Why you talk of the love, and grace, and tenderness, and faithfulness of Christ, why do you not say the like of the Spirit? Was ever love like his, that he should visit us? Was ever mercy like his, that he should bear with our ill manners, though constantly repeated by us? Was ever faithfulness like his, that multitudes of sins cannot drive him away? Was ever power like his, that overcometh all our iniquities, and yet leads us safely on, though hosts of foes within and without would rob us of our Christian life?

"Oh, the love of the Spirit I sing
By whom is redemption applied."
And unto his name be glory for ever and ever.

II. This brings me to the second point. Here we have another reason why we should not grieve the Spirit. IT IS BY THE HOLY SPIRIT WE ARE SEALED. "BY whom we are sealed unto the day of redemption." I shall be very brief here. The Spirit himself is expressed as the seal, even as he himself is directly said to be the pledge of our inheritance. The sealing, I think, has a three-fold meaning. It is a sealing of attestation or confirmation.

I want to know whether I am truly a child of God. The Spirit itself also beareth witness with my spirit that I am born of God. I have the writings, the title-deeds of the inheritance that is to come—I want to know whether those are valid, whether they are true, or whether they are mere counterfeits written out by that old scribe of hell, Master Presumption and Carnal Security. How am I to know? I look for the seal. After that we have believed on the Son of God, the Father seals us as his children, by the gift of the Holy Ghost. "Now he which hath anointed us is God, who also hath sealed us, and given the earnest of the Spirit in our hearse." No faith is genuine which does not bear the seal of the Spirit. No love, no hope can ever save us, except it be sealed with the Spirit of God, for whatever hath not his seal upon it is spurious. Faith that is unsealed may be a poison, it may be presumption; but faith that is sealed by the Spirit is true, real, genuine faith. Never be content, my dear hearers, unless you are sealed, unless you are sure, by the inward witness and testimony of the Holy Ghost, that you have been begotten again unto a lively hope by the resurrection of Jesus Christ from the dead. It is possible for a man to know infallibly that he is secure of heaven. He may not only hope so, but he may know it beyond a doubt, and he may know it thus,—by being able with the eye of faith to see the seal, the broad stamp of the Holy Spirit set upon his own character and experience. It is a seal of attestation.

In the next place, it is a sealing of appropriation. When men put their mark upon an article, it is to show that it is their own. The farmer brands his tools that they may not be stolen. They are his. The shepherd marks his sheep that they may be recognized as belonging to his flock. The king himself puts his broad arrow upon everything that is his property. So the Holy Spirit puts the broad arm of God upon the hearts of all his people. He seals us. "Thou shalt be mine," saith the Lord, "in the day when I make up my jewels." And then the Spirit puts God's seal upon us to signify that we are God's reserved inheritance—his peculiar people, the portion in which his soul delighteth.

But, again, by sealing is meant preservation. Men seal up that which they wish to have preserved, and when a document is sealed it becomes valid henceforth. Now, it is by the Spirit of God that the Christian is sealed, that he is kept, he is preserved, sealed unto the day of redemption—sealed until Christ comes fully to redeem the bodies of his saints by raising them from the death, and fully to redeem the world by purging it from sin, and making it a kingdom unto himself in righteousness. We shall hold on our way, we shall be saved. The chosen seed cannot be lost they must be brought home at last, but how? By the sealing of the Spirit. Apart from that they perish, they are undone. When the last general fire shall blaze out, everything that has not the seal of the Spirit on it, shall be burned up. But the men upon whose forehead is the seal shall be preserved. They shall be safe "amid the wreck of matter and the crash of worlds." Their spirits, mounting above the flames shall dwell with Christ eternally, and with that same seal in their forehead upon Mount Zion, they shall sing the everlasting song of gratitude and praise. I say this is the second reason why we should love the Spirit and why we should not grieve him.

III. I come now to the third part of my discourse, namely, THE GRIEVING OF THE SPIRIT, How may we grieve him,—what will be the sad result of grieving him—if we have grieved him, how may we bring him back again? How may we grieve the Spirit? I am now, mark you, speaking of those who love the Lord Jesus Christ. The Spirit of God is in your heart, and it is very, very easy indeed to grieve him, Sin is as easy as it is wicked. You may grieve him by impure thoughts. He cannot bear sin. If you indulge in lascivious expressions, or if even you allow imagination to coat upon any lascivious act, or if your heart goes after covetousness, if you set your heart upon anything that is evil, the Spirit of God will be grieved, for thus I hear him speaking of himself. "I love this man, I want to have his heart, and yet be is entertaining these filthy lusts. His thoughts, instead of running after me, and after Christ, and after the Father, are running after the temptations that are in the world through lust." And then his Spirit is grieved. He sorrows in his soul because he knows what sorrow these things must bring to our souls. We grieve him yet more if we indulge in outward acts of sin. Then is he sometimes so grieved that he takes his flight for a season, for the dove will not dwell in our hearts if we take loathsome carrion in there. A cleanly being is the dove, and we must not strew the place which the dove frequents with filth and mire, if we do he will fly elsewhere. If we commit sin if we openly bring disgrace upon our religion, if we tempt others to go into iniquity by our evil example, it is not long before the Holy Spirit will begin to grieve. Again, if we neglect prayer, if our closet door is cob-webbed, if we forget to read the Scriptures, if the leaves of our Bible are almost stuck together by neglect, if we never seek to do any good in the world, if we live merely for ourselves and not to Christ, then the Holy Spirit will be grieved, for thus he saith, "They have forsaken me, they have left the fountain of waters, they have hewn unto themselves broken cisterns." I think I now see the Spirit of God grieving, when you are sitting down to read a novel and there is your Bible unread. Perhaps you take down some book of travels, and you forget that you have got a more precious book of travels in the Acts of the Apostles, and in the story of your blessed Lord and Master. You have no time for prayer, but the Spirit sees you very active about worldly things, and having many hours to spare for relaxation and amusement. And then he is grieved because he sees that you love worldly things better than you love him. His spirit is grieved within him; take care that he does not go away from you, for it will be a pitiful thing for you if he leaves you to yourself. Again, ingratitude tends to grieve him. Nothing cut a man to the heart more than after having done his utmost for another, he turns round and repays him with ingratitude or insult. If we do not want to be thanked, at least we do love to know that there is thankfulness in the heart upon which we have conferred a boon, and when the Holy Spirit looks into our soul and sees little love to Christ, no gratitude to him for all he has done for us, then is he grieved.

Again, the Holy Spirit is exceedingly grieved by our unbelief. When we distrust the promise he hath given and applied, when we doubt the power or the affection of our blessed Lord, then the Spirit saith within himself—"They doubt my fidelity, they distrust my power, they say Jesus is not able to save unto the uttermost, thus again is the Spirit grieved. Oh, I wish the Spirit had an advocate here this morning, that could speak in better terms than I can. I have a theme that overmasters me, I seem to grieve for him; but I cannot make you grieve, nor tell out the grief I feel. In my own soul I keep saying, "Oh, this is just what you have done—you have grieved him." Let me make a full and frank confession even before you all. I know that too often, I as well as you have grieved the Holy Spirit. Much within us has made that sacred dove to mourn, and my marvel is, that he has not taken his flight from us and left us utterly to ourselves.

Now suppose the Holy Spirit is grieved, what is the effect produced upon us? When the Spirit is grieved first, he bears with us. He is grieved again and again, and again and again, and still he bears with it all. But at last, his grief becomes so excessive, that he says, "I will suspend my operations; I will begone; I will leave life behind me, but my own actual presence I will take away. And when the Spirit of God goes away from the soul and suspends all his operations what a miserable state we are in. He suspends his instructions; we read the word, we cannot understand it; we go to our commentaries, they cannot tell us the meaning; we fall on our knees and ask to be taught, but we get no answer, we learn nothing. He suspends his comfort; we used to dance, like David before the ark, and now we sit like Job in the ash-pit, and scrape our ulcers with a potsherd. There was a time when his candle shone round about us, but now he is gone; he has left us in the blackness of darkness. Now, he takes from us all spiritual power. Once we could do all things; now we can do nothing. We could slay the Philistines, and lay them heaps upon heaps, but now Delilah can deceive us, and our eyes are put out and we are made to grind in the mill. We go preaching, and there is no pleasure in preaching, and no good follows it. We go to our tract distributing, and our Sunday-school, we might almost as well be at home. There is the machinery there, but there is no love. There is the intention to do good, or perhaps not even that, but alas! there is no power to accomplish the intention. The Lord has withdrawn himself, his light, his joy, his comfort, his spiritual power, all are gone. And then all our graces flag. Our graces are much like the flower called the Hydrangia, when it has plenty of water it blooms, but as soon as moisture fails, the leaves drop down at once. And so when the Spirit goes away, faith shuts up its flowers; no perfume is exhaled. Then the fruit of our love begins to rot and drops from the tree; then the sweet buds of our hope become frostbitten, and they die. Oh, what a sad thing it is to lose the Spirit. Have you never, my brethren, been on your knees and have been conscious that the Spirit of God was not with you, and what awful work it has been to groan, and cry, and sigh, and yet go away again, and no light to shine upon the promises, not so much as a ray of light through the chink of the dungeon. All forsaken, forgotten, and forlorn, you are almost driven to despair. You sing with Cowper:—

"What peaceful hours I once enjoyed,
How sweet their memory still!
But they have left an aching void,
The world can never fill.
Return, thou sacred dove, return,
Sweet messenger of rest,
I hate the sins that made thee mourn,
And drove thee from my breast.
The dearest idol I have known,
Whate'er that idol be,
Help me to tear it from its throne,
And worship only thee."

Ah! sad enough it is to have the Spirit drawn from us. But, my brethren, I am about to say something with the utmost charity, which, perhaps, may look severe, but, nevertheless, I must say it. The churches of the present day are very much in the position of those who have grieved the Spirit of God; for the Spirit deals with churches just as it does with individuals. Of these late years how little has God wrought in the midst of his churches. Throughout England, at least some four or five years ago, an almost universal torpor had fallen upon the visible body of Christ. There was a little action, but it was spasmodic; there was no real vitality. Oh! how few sinners were brought to Christ, how empty had our places of worship become; our prayer-meetings were dwindling away to nothing, and our church meetings were mere matters of farce. You know right well that this is the case with many London churches to this day; and there be some that do not mourn about it. They go up to their accustomed place, and the minister prays, and the people either sleep with their eyes or else with their hearts, and they go out, and there is never a soul saved. The pool of baptism is seldom stirred; but the saddest part of all is this, the churches are willing to have it so. They are not earnest to get a revival of religion. We have been doing something, the church at large has been doing something. I will not just now put my finger upon what the sin is, but there has been something done which has driven the Spirit of God from us. He is grieved, and he is gone. He is present with us here, I thank his name, he is still visible in our midst. He has not left us. Though we have been as unworthy as others, yet has he given us a long outpouring of his presence. These five years or more, we have had a revival which is not to be exceeded by any revival upon the face of the earth. Without cries or shoutings, without fallings down or swooning, steadily God adds to this church numbers upon numbers, so that your minister's heart is ready to break with very joy when he thinks how manifestly the Spirit of God is with us. But brethren, we must not be content with this, we want to see the Spirit poured out on all churches. Look at the great gatherings that there were in St. Paul's, and Westminster Abbey, and Exeter Hall, and other places, how was it that no good was done, or so very little? I have watched with anxious eye, and I have never from that day forth heard but of one conversion, and that in St. James' Hall, from all these services. Strange it seems. The blessing may have come in larger measure than we know, but not in so large a measure as we might have expected, if the Spirit of God had been present with all the ministers. Oh would that we may live to see greater things than we have ever seen yet. Go home to your houses, humble yourselves before God, ye members of Christ's church, and cry aloud that he will visit his church, and that he would open the windows of heaven and pour out his grace upon his thirsty hill of Zion, that nations may be born in a day, that sinners may be saved by thousands—that Zion may travail and may bring forth children. Oh! there are signs and tokens of a coming revival. We have heard but lately of a good work among the Ragged School boys of St. Giles's, and our soul has been glad on account of that; and the news from Ireland comes to us like good tidings, not from a far country, but from a sister province of the kingdom. Let us cry aloud to the Holy Spirit, who is certainly grieved with his church, and let us purge our churches of everything that is contrary to his Word and to sound doctrine, and then the Spirit will return, and his power shall be manifest.

And now, in conclusion, there may be some of you here who have lost the visible presence of Christ with you; who have in fact so grieved the Spirit that he has gone. It is a mercy for you to know that the Spirit of God never leaves his people finally; he leaves them for chastisement, but not for damnation. He sometimes leaves them that they may get good by knowing their own weakness, but he will not leave them finally to perish. Are you in a state of backsliding, declension, and coldness? Hearken to me for a moment, and God bless the words. Brother, stay not a moment in a condition so perilous; be not easy for a single second in the absence of the Holy Ghost. I beseech you use every means by which that Spirit may be brought back to you. Once more, let me tell you distinctly what the means are. Search out for the sin that has grieved the Spirit, give it up, slay that sin upon the spot; repent with tears and sighs; continue in prayer, and never rest satisfied until the Holy Ghost comes back to you. Frequent an earnest ministry, get much with earnest saints, but above all, be much in prayer to God, and let your daily cry be, "Return, return, O Holy Spirit return, and dwell in my soul." Oh, I beseech you be not content till that prayer is heard, for you have become weak as water, and faint and empty while the Spirit has been away from you. Oh! it may be there are some here this morning with whom the Spirit has been striving during the past week. Oh yield to him, resist him not; grieve him not, but yield to him. Is he saying to you now "Turn to Christ?" Listen to him, obey him, he moves you. Oh I beseech you do not despise him. Have you resisted him many a time, then take care you do not again, for there may come a last time when the Spirit may say, "I will go unto my rest,

I will not return unto him, the ground is accursed, it shall be given up to barrenness." Oh I hear the word of the gospel, ere ye separate, for the Spirit speaketh effectually to you now in this short sentence—"Repent and be converted everyone of you, that your sins may be blotted out when the times of refreshing shall come from the presence of the Lord," and hear this solemn sentence, "He that believeth in the Lord Jesus and is baptized, shall be saved; but he that believeth not shall be damned." May the Lord grant that we may not grieve the Holy Spirit. Amen.

Chapter 9
THE HOLY SPIRIT AND THE ONE CHURCH

"These be they who separate themselves, sensual, having not the Spirit."—Jude 1:19.

When a farmer comes to thrash out his wheat, and get it ready for the market there are two things that he desires—that there may be plenty of it, of the right sort, and that when he takes it to market, he may be able to carry a clean sample there. He does not look upon the quantity alone; for what is the chaff to the wheat? He would rather have a little clean than he would have a great heap containing a vast quantity of chaff, but less of the precious corn. On the other hand, he would not so winnow his wheat as to drive away any of the good grain, and so make the quantity less than it need to be. He wants to have as much as possible—to have as little loss as possible in the winnowing, and yet to have it as well winnowed as may be. Now, that is what I desire for Christ's Church, and what every Christian will desire. We wish Christ's church to be as large as possible. God forbid that by any of our winnowing, we should ever cast away one of the precious sons of Zion. When we rebuke sharply, we would be anxious lest the rebuke should fall where it is not needed, and should bruise and hurt the feelings of any who God hath chosen. But on the other hand, we have no wish to see the church multiplied at the expense of its purity. We do not wish to have a charity so large that it takes in chaff as well as wheat: we wish to be just charitable enough to use the fan thoroughly to purge God's floor, but yet charitable enough to pick up the most shrivelled ear of wheat, to preserve it for the Master's sake, who is the husbandman. I trust, in preaching this morning, God may help me so to discern between the precious and the vile that I may say nothing uncharitable, which would cut off any of God's people from being part of his true and living and visible church; and yet at the same time I pray that I may not speak so loosely, and so without God's direction, as to embrace any in the arms of Christian affection whom the Lord hath not received in the eternal covenant of his love.

Our text suggests to us three things: first, an inquiry—Have we the Spirit? secondly, a caution—if we have not the spirit we are sensual; thirdly, a suspicion—there are many persons that separate themselves. Our suspicion concerning them is, that notwithstanding their extra-superfine profession, they are sensual, not having the Spirit; for our text says, "These be they who separate themselves, sensual, having not the Spirit."

I. First, then, our text suggests AN INQUIRY—Have we the Spirit? This is an inquiry so important, that the philosopher may well suspend all his investigations to find an answer to this question on his own personal account. All the great debates of politics, all the most engrossing subjects of human discussion, may well stop to-day, and give us pause to ask ourselves the solemn question—"Have I the Spirit?" For this question does not deal with any externals of religion, but it deals with religion in its most vital point. He that hath the Spirit, although he be wrong in fifty things, being right in this, is saved; he that hath not the Spirit, be he never so orthodox, be his creed as correct as Scripture-ay and in his morals outwardly as pure as the law, is still unsaved; he is destitute of the essential part of salvation—the Spirit of God dwelling in him.

To help us to answer this question, I shall try to set forth the effects of the Spirit in our hearts under sundry Scriptural metaphors. Have I the Spirit? I reply, And what is the operation of the, Spirit? How am I to discern it? Now the Spirit operates in divers ways, all of them mysterious, and supernatural, all of them bearing the real marks of his own power, and having certain signs following whereby they may be discovered and recognised.

1. The first work of the Spirit in the heart is a work during which the Spirit is compared to the wind. You remember that when our Saviour spoke to Nicodemus he represented the first work of the Spirit in the heart as being like the wind, "which bloweth where it listeth;" "even so;" saith he, "is every one that is born of the Spirit." Now you know that the wind is a most mysterious thing; and although there be certain definitions of it which pretend to be explanations of the phenomenon, yet they certainly leave the great question of how the wind blows, and what is the cause of its blowing in a certain direction, where it was before. Breath within us, wind without us, all motions of air, are to us mysterious. And the renewing work of the Spirit in the heart is exceedingly mysterious. It is possible that at this moment the Spirit of God may be breathing into some of the thousand hearts before me; yet it would be blasphemous if any one should ask, "Which way went the

Spirit from God to such a heart? How entered it there?" And it would be foolish for a person who is under the operation of the Spirit to ask how it operates: thou knowest not where is the storehouse of the thunder; thou knowest not where the clouds are balanced; neither canst thou know how the Spirit goeth forth from the Most High and enters into the heart of man. It may be, that during a sermon two men are listening to the same truth; one of them hears as attentively as the other and remembers as much of it; the other is melted to tears or moved with solemn thoughts; but the one though equally attentive, sees nothing in the sermon, except, maybe, certain important truths well set forth; as for the other, his heart is broken within him and his soul is melted. Ask me how it is that the same truth has an effect upon the one, and not upon his fellow: I reply, because the mysterious Spirit of the living God goes with the truth to one heart and not to the other. The one only feels the force of truth, and that may be strong enough to make him tremble, like Felix; but the other feels the Spirit going with the truth, and that renews the man, regenerates him, and causes him to pass into that gracious condition which is called the state of salvation. This change takes place instantaneously. It is as miraculous a change as any miracle of which we read in Scripture. It is supremely supernatural. It may be mimicked, but no imitation of it can be true and real. Men may pretend to be regenerated without the Spirit, but regenerated they cannot be. It is a change so marvellous that the highest attempts of man can never reach it. We may reason as long as we please, but we cannot reason ourselves into regeneration; we may meditate till our hairs are grey with study; but we cannot meditate ourselves into the new birth. That is worked in us by the sovereign will of God alone.

"The Spirit, like some heavenly wind,
Blows on the sons of flesh,
Inspires us with a heavenly mind,
And forms the man afresh."

But ask the man how: he cannot tell you. Ask him when: he may recognize the time, but as to the manner thereof he knoweth no more of it than you do. It is to him a mystery.

You remember the story of the valley of vision. Ezekiel saw dry bones lying scattered here and there in the valley. The command came to Ezekiel, "Say to:these dry bones, live." He said, "Live," and the bones came together, "bone to his bone, and flesh came upon them;" but as yet they did not live.

"Prophesy, son of man; say to the wind, breathe upon these slain, that they may live." They looked just like life: there was flesh and blood there; there were the eyes and hands and feet; but when Ezekiel had spoken there was a mysterious something given which men call life, and it was given in a mysterious way, like the blowing of the wind. It is even so to-day. Unconverted and ungodly persons may be very, moral and excellent; they are like the dry bones, when they are put together and clothed with flesh and blood. But to make them live spiritually it needs the divine afflatus from the breath of the Almighty, the divine pneuma, the divine Spirit, the divine wind should blow on them, and then they would live. Say, my hearer, hast thou ever had any supernatural influence on thine Heart? For if not I may seem to be harsh with thee, but I am faithful: if thou hast never had more than nature in thy heart, thou art "in the gall of bitterness and in the bonds of iniquity." Nay, sir, sneer not at that utterance; it is as true as this Bible, for tis from this Bible it was taken, and for proof thereof hear thou me. "except a man be born again (from above) of water and of the Spirit, he cannot see the kingdom of God." What sayest thou to that? It is in vain for thee to talk of making thyself to be born again; thou canst not be born again except by the Spirit, and thou must perish, unless thou art. You see, then, the first effect of the Spirit, and by that you may answer the question.

2. In the next place, the Spirit in the word of God is often compared to fire. After the Spirit, like the wind, has made the dead sinner live, then comes the Spirit like fire. Now, fire has a searching and tormenting power. It is purifying, but it purifies by a terrible process. Now, after the Holy Spirit has given us the life of Christianity, there immediately begins a burning in our heart: the Lord searches and tries our reins, and lights a candle within our spirits which discovers the wickedness of our nature, and the loathsomeness of our iniquities. Say, my hearer, dost thou know anything about that fire in thine heart? For if not, thou hast not yet received the Spirit. To explain what I mean, let me just tell a piece of my own experience, by way of illustrating the fiery effects of the Spirit. I lived careless and thoughtless; I could indulge in sin as well as others, and did do so. Sometimes my conscience pricked me, but not enough to make me cease from vice. I could indulge in transgression, and I could love it: not so much as others loved it—mine early training would not let me do that—but still enough to prove that my heart was debased and corrupt. Once on a time something more than conscience pricked me: I knew not then what it was. I was like Samuel, when the Lord

called him; I heard the voice, but I knew not whence it came. A stirring began in my heart, and I began to feel that in the sight of God I was a lost, ruined, and condemned sinner. That conviction I could not shake off. Do what I might it followed me. If I sought to amuse my mind and take it off from serious thoughts it was of no use; I was obliged still to carry about with me a heavy burden on my back. I went to my bed, and there I dreamed about hell, and about "the wrath to come." I woke up, and this dreary nightmare, this incubus, still brooded on me. What could I do? I renounced first one vicious habit, then another: it mattered not; all this was like pulling one firebrand from a flame, that fed itself with blazing forests. Do what I might, my conscience found no rest. Up to the house of God I went to hear the gospel: there was no gospel for me; the fire burned but the more fiercely, and the very breath of the gospel seemed to fan the flame. Away I went to my chamber and my closet to pray: the heavens were like brass, and the windows of the sky were barred against me. No answer could I get; the fire burned more vehemently. Then I thought, "I would not live always; would God I had never been born!" But I dared not die, for there was hell when I was dead; and I dared not live, for life had become intolerable. Still the fire blazed right vehemently; till at last I came to this resolve: "If there be salvation in Christ, I will have it. I have nothing of my own to trust to; I do this hour, O God, renounce my sin, and renounce my own righteousness too." And the fire blazed again, and burned up all my good works, ay, and my sins with them. And then I saw that all this burning was to bring me to Christ. And oh! the joy and gladness of my heart, when Jesus came and sprinkled water on the flame, and said, "I have bought thee with my blood; put thy trust in me; I will do for thee what thou canst not do for thyself; I will take thy sins away; I will clothe thee with a spotless robe of righteousness; I will guide thee all thy journey through, and land thee at last in heaven." Say, my dear hearer, Dost know anything about the Spirit of burning? For if not, again I say, I am not harsh, I am but true; if thou hast never felt this, thou knowest not the Spirit.

3. To proceed a little further. When the Spirit has thus quickened the soul and convinced it of sin, then he comes under another metaphor. He comes under the metaphor of oil. The Holy Spirit is very frequently in Scripture compared to oil. "Thou anointest mine head with oil; my cup runneth over." Ah! brethren, though the beginning of the Spirit is by fire, it does not end there. We may be first of all convinced and brought to Christ by misery; but

when we get to Christ there is no misery in him, and our sorrow results from not getting close enough to him. The Holy Spirit comes, like the good Samaritan, and pours in the oil and the wine. And oh! what oil it is with which he anoints our head, and with which he heals our wounds! How soft the liniments which he binds round our bruises! How blessed the eye-salve with which he anoints our eyes! How heavenly the ointment with which he binds up our sores, and wounds, and bruises, and makes us whole, and sets our feet upon a rock, and establishes our goings! The Spirit, after he has convinced, begins to comfort; and ye that have felt the comforting power of the Holy Spirit, will bear me witness there is no comforter like him that is the Paraclete. Oh! bring hither the music, the voice of song, and the sound of harps; they are both as vinegar upon nitre to him that hath a heavy heart. Bring me here the enchantments of the magic world, and all the enjoyments of its pleasures; they do but torment the soul and prick it with many thorns. But oh! Spirit of the living God, when thou dost blow upon the heart, there is not a wave of that tempestuous sea which does not sleep for ever when thou biddest it be still; there is not one single breath of the proud hurricane and tempest which doth not cease to howl and which doth not lie still, when thou sayest to it, "Peace be unto thee; thy sins are forgiven thee." Say, do you know the Spirit under the figure of oil? Have you felt him at work in your spirits, comforting you, anointing your head, making you glad, and causing you to rejoice?

There are many people that never felt this. They hope they are religious; but their religion never makes them happy. There are scores of professors who have just enough religion to make them miserable. Let them be afraid that they have any religion at all; for religion makes people happy; when it has its full sway with man it makes him glad. It may begin in agony, but it does not end there. Say, hast thou ever had thine heart leaping for joy? Hath thy lip ever warbled songs of ecstatic praise? Doth thine eye ever flash the fire of joy? If these things be not so, I fear lest thou art still without God, and without Christ; for where the Spirit comes, his fruits are, joy in the Spirit, and peace, and love, and confidence, and assurance for ever.

4. Bear with me once more. I have to show you one more figure of the Spirit, and by that also you will be able to ascertain whether you are under his operation. When the Spirit has acted as wind, as fire, and as oil, he then acts like water. We are told that we are "born again of water and of the Spirit." Now I do not think you foolish enough to need that I should say that

no water, either of immersion or of sprinkling, can in the least degree operate in the salvation of a soul. There may be some few poor creatures, whose heads were put on their shoulders the wrong way, who still believe that a few drops of water from a priest's hands can regenerate souls. There may be such a few, but I hope the race will soon die out. We trust that the day will come when all those gentry will have no "other Gospel" to preach in our churches, but will have clean gone over to Rome, and when that terrible plague-spot upon the Protestant Church, called Puseyism, will have been cut out like a cancer, and torn out by its very roots. The sooner we get rid of that the better; and whenever we hear of any of them going over to Rome, let them go—I wish we could as easily get rid of the devil, they may go together—we do not want either of them in the Protestant Church, anyhow. But the Holy Spirit when he comes in the heart comes like water. That is to say, he comes to purify the soul. He that is to-day as foul a liver as he was before his pretended conversion is a hypocrite and a liar; he that this day loveth sin and liveth in it just as he was wont to do, let him know that the truth is not in him, but he hath received the strong delusion to believe a lie: God's people are a holy people; God's Spirit works by love, and purifies the soul. Once let it get into our hearts, and it will have no rest till it has turned every sin out. God's Holy Spirit and man's sin cannot live together peaceably; they may both be in the same heart, but they cannot both reign there, nor can they both be quiet there; for "the Spirit lusteth against the flesh, and the flesh lusteth against the Spirit;" they cannot rest, but there will be a perpetual warring in the soul, so that the Christian will have to cry, "O wretched man that I am! who shall deliver me from the body of this death?" But in due time the Spirit will drive out all sin, and will present us blameless before the throne of his Majesty with exceeding great joy.

Now, my hearer, answer thou this question for thyself, and not for another man. Hast thou received this Spirit? Answer me, anyhow; if it be with a scoff, answer me; if thou sneerest and sayest, "I know nothing of your enthusiastic rant," be it so, sir; say, nay, then. It may be thou carest not to reply at all. I beseech thee do not put away my entreaty. Yes or no. Hast thou received the Spirit? "Sir no man can find fault with my character; I believe I shall enter heaven through my own virtues." It is not the question, sir. Hast thou received the Spirit? All that thou sayest thou mayest have done; but if thou hast left the other undone, and hast not received the Spirit, it will go ill with thee at last. Hast thou had a supernatural operation upon thine own heart? Hast thou been made a new man in Christ Jesus! For if not, depend on it, as God's Word is true, thou art out of Christ, and dying as thou art thou wilt be shut out of heaven, be thou who thou mayest and what thou mayest.

II. Thus, I have tried to help you to answer the first question—the inquiry, Have we received the Spirit? And this brings me to the CAUTION. He that has not received the Spirit is said to be sensual. Oh, what a gulf there is between the least Christian and the greatest moralist! What a wide distinction there is between the greatest professor destitute of grace, and the least of God's believers who has grace in his heart. As great a difference as there is between light and darkness between death and life, between heaven and hell, is there between a saint and a sinner; for mark, my text says, in no very polite phrase, that if we have not the Spirit we are sensual. "Sensual!" says one; "well, I am not converted man—I don t pretend to be; but I am not sensual." Well, friend, and it is very likely that you are not—not in the common acceptation of the term sensual; but understand that this word, in the Greek, really means what an English word like this would mean, if we had such a one—soulish. We have not such a word—we want such a one. There is a great distinction between mere animals and men, because man hath a soul, and the mere animal hath none. There is another distinction between mere men and a converted man. The converted man hath the Spirit—the unconverted man hath none; he is a soulish man—not a spiritual man; he has got no further than mere nature and has no inheritance in the spiritual kingdom of grace. Strange it is that soulish and sensual should after all mean the same! Friend, thou hast not the Spirit. Then thou art nothing better—be thou what thou art, or whatsoever thou mayest be—than the fall of Adam left thee. That is to say, thou art a fallen creature, having only capacities to live here in sin, and to live for ever in torment; but thou hast not the capacity to live in heaven at all, for thou hast no Spirit; and therefore thou art unable to know or enjoy spiritual things. And mark you, a man may be in this state, and be a sensual man, and yet he may have all the virtues that could grace a Christian; but with all these, if he has not the Spirit, he has got not an inch further than where Adam's fall left him—that is, condemned and under the curse. Ay, and he may attend to religion with all his might—he may take the sacrament, and be baptized, and may be the most devout professor; but if he hath not the Spirit he hath not started a solitary inch from where he was, for he is still in "the bonds of iniquity," a lost soul. Nay, further, he may pick up religious phrases till he may talk very fast about religion; he may read biographies till he seems to be a deep taught child of God; he may be able to write an article upon the deep experience of a believer; but if this experience be not his own, if he hath not received it by the Spirit of the living God, he is still nothing more than a carnal man, and heaven is to him a place to which there is no entrance. Nay, further, he might go so far as to become a minister of the gospel, and a successful minister too, and God may bless the word that he preaches to the salvation of sinners, but unless he has received the Spirit, be he as eloquent as Apollos, and as earnest as Paul, he is nothing more than a mere soulish man, without capacity for spiritual things.

Nay, to crown all, he might even have the power of working miracles, as Judas had—he might even be received into the church as a believer, as was Simon Magus, and after all that, though he had cast out devils, though he had healed the sick, though he had worked miracles, he might have the gates of heaven shut in his teeth, if he had not received the Spirit. For this is the essential thing, without which all others are in vain—the reception of the Spirit of the living God. It is a searching truth, is it not, my friends? Do not run away from it. If I am preaching to you falsehood, reject it; but if this be a truth which I can substantiate by Scripture, I beseech you, rest not till you have answered this question: Hast thou the Spirit, living, dwelling, working in thy heart?

III. This brings me, in the third place, to THE SUSPICION. How singular that "separation" should be the opposite of having the Spirit. Hark! I hear a gentle man saying, "Oh! I like to hear you preach smartly and sharply; I am persuaded, sir, there are a great many people in the church that ought not to be there; and so I, because there is such a corrupt mixture in the church, have determined not to join anywhere at all. I do not think that the Church of Christ now a days is at all clean and pure enough to allow of my joining with it. At least, sir, I did join a church once, but I made such a deal of noise in it they were very glad when I went away. And now I am just like David's men; I am one that is in debt and discontented, and I go round to hear all new preachers that arise. I have heard you now these three months; I mean to go and hear some one else in a very little time if you do not say something to flatter me. But I am quite sure I am one of God's special elect. I don't join any church because a church is not good enough for me; I don't become a member of any denomination, because they are all wrong, every one of them." Hark ye brother, I have something to tell you, that will not please you. "These be they that separate themselves, sensual, having not the Spirit."

I hope you enjoy the text: it certainly belongs to you, above every man in the world. "These be they who separate themselves, sensual, having not the Spirit." When I read this over I thought to myself, there be some who say, "Well, you are a dissenter, how do you make this agreeable with the text, 'These be they who separate themselves;' " you are separated from the Church of England. Ah, my friends, that a man may be, and be all the better for it; but the separation here intended is separation from the one universal Church of Christ. The Church of England was not known in Jude's day: so the apostle did not allude to that. "These be they who separate themselves,"—that is from the Church of Christ; from the great universal body of the elect. Moreover, let us just say one thing. We did not separate ourselves—we were turned out. Dissenters did not separate themselves from the Church of England, from the Episcopal church; but when the Act of Uniformity was passed, they were turned out of their pulpits. Our forefathers were as sound Churchmen as any in the world, but they could not take in all the errors of the Prayer Book, and they were therefore hounded to their graves by the intolerance of the conforming professors. So they did not separate themselves. Moreover, we do not separate ourselves. There is not a Christian beneath the scope of God's heaven from whom I am separated. At the Lord's table I always invite all Churches to come and sit down and commune with us. If any man were to tell me that I am separate from the Episcopalian, the Presbyterian, or the Methodist, I would tell him he did not know me, for I love them with a pure heart fervently, and I am not separate from them. I may hold different views from them, and in that point truly I may be said to be separate; but I am not separate in heart, I will work with them—I will work with them heartily; nay, though my Church of England brother sends me in, as he has done, a summons to pay a church-rate that I cannot in conscience pay, I will love him still; and if he takes chairs and tables it matters not—I will love him for all that; and if there be a ragged-school or anything else for which I can work with him to promote the glory of God, therein will I unite with him with all my heart. I think this bears rather hard on our friends—the Strict Communion Baptists. I should not like to say anything hard against them, for they are about the best people in the world, but they really do separate themselves from the great body of Christ's people. The Spirit of the living God will not let them do this really, but they do it professedly. They separate themselves from the great Universal Church. They say they will not commune with it; and if any one comes to their table who has not been baptized, they turn him away. They "separate," certainly. I do not believe it is willful schism that makes them thus act; but at the same time I think the old man within has some hand in it.

Oh, how my heart loves the doctrine of the one church. The nearer I get to my Master in prayer and communion, the closer am I knit to all his disciples. The more I see of my own errors and failings, the more ready am I to deal gently with them that I believe to be erring. The pulse of Christ's body is communion; and woe to the church that seeks to cure the ills of Christ's body by stopping its pulse. I think it sin to refuse to commune with anyone who is a member of the Church of our Lord Jesus Christ. I desire this morning to preach the unity of Christ's church. I have sought to use the fan to blow away the chaff. I have said no man belongs to Christ's church unless he has the Spirit; but, if he hath the Spirit, woe be to the man that separates himself from him. Oh! I should think myself grossly in fault if at the foot of these stairs I should meet a truly converted child of God, who called himself a Primitive Methodist, or a Wesleyan. or a Churchman, or an Independent, and I should say, "No, sir, you do not agree with me on certain points; I believe you are a child of God, but I will have nothing to do with you." I should then think that this text would bear very hard on me. "These be they who separate themselves, sensual, having not the Spirit." But would we do so, beloved? No, we would give them both our hands, and say, God speed to you in your journey to heaven; so long as you have got the Spirit we are one family, and we will not be separate from one another. God grant the day may come when every wall of separation shall be beaten down! See how to this day we are separate. There! you will find a Baptist who could not say a good word to a Poedo-Baptist if you were to give him a world. You find to this day Episcopalians who hate that ugly word, "Dissent;" and it is enough for them that a Dissenter has done a thing; they will not do it then, be it never so good.

Ah! and furthermore, there are some to be found in the Church of England that will not only hate dissent, but hate one another into the bargain. Men are to be found that cannot let brother ministers of their own church preach in their parish. What an anachronism such men are! They would seem to have been sent into the world in our time purely by mistake. Their proper era would have been the time of the dark ages. If they had lived then, what fine Bonners they would have made! What splendid fellows they would have been to have helped to poke the fire in Smithfield! But they are quite out of date in these times, and I look upon such a curious clergyman in the same way that I do upon a Dodo—as an extraordinary animal whose race is almost, if not quite extinct. Well, you may look, and look and wonder. The animal will be extinct soon. It will not be long, I trust, before not only the Church of England shall love itself, but when all who love the Lord Jesus shall be ready to preach in each other's pulpits, preaching the same truth, holding the same faith, and mightily contending for it. Then shall the world "see how these Christians love one another; " and then shall it be known in heaven that Christ s kingdom has come, and that his will is about to be done on earth as it is in heaven.

My hearer, dost thou belong to the church? For out of the church there is no salvation. But mark what the church is. It is not the Episcopalian, Baptist, or Presbyterian: the church is a company of men who have received the Spirit. If thou canst not say thou hast the Spirit, go thy way and tremble; go thy way and think of thy lost condition; and may Jesus by his Spirit so bless thee, that thou mayest be led to renounce thy works and ways with grief, and fly to him who died upon the cross, and find a shelter there from the wrath of God.

I may have said some rough things this morning, but I am not given much to cutting and trimming, and I do not suppose I shall begin to learn that art now. If the thing is untrue, it is with you to reject it; if it be true, at your own peril reject what God stamps with divine authority. May the blessing of the Father, the Son, and the Holy Spirit rest upon the one church of Israel's one Jehovah. Amen and Amen.

Chapter 10
THE POWER OF THE HOLY GHOST

"The power of the Holy Ghost."—Romans 15:13.

Power is the special and peculiar prerogative of God, and God alone. "Twice have I heard this; that power belongeth unto God." God is God; and power belongeth to him. If he delegates a portion of it to his creatures, yet still it is his power. The sun, although he is "like a bridegroom coming out of his chamber, and rejoiceth as a strong man to run his race," yet has no power to perform his motions except as God directs him. The stars, although they travel in their orbits, and none could stay them, yet have neither might nor force, except that which God daily infuses into them. The tall archangel, near his throne, who outshines a comet in its blaze, though he is one of those who excel in strength, and hearken to the voice of the commands of God, yet has no might except that which his Maker gives to him. As for Leviathan, who so maketh the sea to boil like a pot, that one would think the deep were hoary; as for Behemoth, who drinketh up Jordan at a draught, and boasteth that he can snuff up rivers; as for those majestic creatures that are found on earth, they owe their strength to him who fashioned their bones of steel, and made their sinews of brass. And when we think of man, if he has might or power, it is so small and insignificant, that we can scarcely call it such; yea, when it is at its greatest—when he sways his sceptre, when he commands hosts, when he rules nations—still the power belongeth unto God; and it is true, "Twice have I heard this, that power belongeth unto God." This exclusive prerogative of God, is to be found in each of the three persons of the glorious Trinity. The Father hath power; for by his word were the heavens made, and all the hosts of them; by his strength all things stand, and through him they fulfil their destiny. The Son hath power; for, like his Father, he is the Creator of all things; "Without him was not anything made that was made," and "by him all things consist." And the Holy Spirit hath power. It is concerning the power of the Holy Ghost that I shall speak this morning; and may you have a practical exemplification of that attribute in your own hearts, when you shall feel that the influence of the Holy Ghost is being poured out upon me, so that I am speaking the words of the living God to your souls, and bestowed upon you when you are feeling the effects of it in your own spirits.

We shall look at the power of the Holy Ghost in three ways this morning. First, the outward and visible displays of it; second, the inward and spiritual manifestations of it; and third, the future and expected works thereof. The power of the Spirit will thus, I trust, be made clearly present to your souls.

I. First, then, we are to view the power of the Spirit in the OUTWARD AND VISIBLE DISPLAYS OF IT. The power of the Sprit has not been dormant; it has exerted itself. Much has been done by the Spirit of God already; more than could have been accomplished by any being except the Infinite, Eternal, Almighty Jehovah, of whom the Holy Spirit is one person. There are four works which are the outward and manifest signs of the power of the Spirit; creation works; resurrection works; works of attestation, or of witness; and works of grace. Of each of these works I shall speak very briefly.

1. First, the Spirit has manifested the omnipotence of his power in creation works; for though not very frequently in Scripture, yet sometimes creation is ascribed to the Holy Ghost, as well as to the Father and the Son. The creation of the heavens above us, is said to be the work of God's Spirit. This you will see at once by referring to the sacred Scriptures, Job 26, 13th verse, "By his Spirit he hath garnished the heavens; his hand hath formed the crooked serpent." All the stars of heaven are said to have been placed aloft by the Spirit, and one particular constellation called the "crooked serpent," is specially pointed out as his handiwork. He looseth the bands of Orion; he bindeth the sweet influences of the Pleiades, and binds Arcturus with his suns. He made all those stars that shine in heaven. The heavens were garnished by his hands, and he formed the crooked serpent by his might. So, also, in those continued acts of creation which are still performed in the world; as the bringing forth of man and animals, their birth and generation. These are ascribed also to the Holy Ghost. If you look at the 104th Psalm, at the 29th verse you will read, "Thou hidest thy face, they are troubled; thou takest away their breath, they die, and return to their dust. Thou sendest forth thy Spirit, they are created; and thou renewest the face of the earth." So that the creation of every man is the work of the Spirit; and the creation of all life, and all flesh-existence in this world, is as much to be ascribed to the power of the Spirit, as the first garnishing of the heavens, or the fashioning

of the crooked serpent. But if you look in the first chapter of Genesis, you will there see more particularly set forth that peculiar operation of power upon the universe which was put forth by the Holy Spirit; you will then discover what was his special work. In the 2d verse of the first chapter of Genesis, we read, "And the earth was without form, and void; and darkness was upon the face of the deep. And the Spirit of God moved upon the face of the waters." We know not how remote the period of the creation of this globe may be—certainly many millions of years before the time of Adam. Our planet has passed through various stages of existence, and different kinds of creatures have lived on its surface, all of which have been fashioned by God. But before that era came, wherein man should be its principal tenant and monarch, the Creator gave up the world to confusion. He allowed the inward fires to burst up from beneath, and melt all the solid matter, so that all kinds of substances were commingled in one vast mass of disorder. The only name you could give to the world, then, was that it was a chaotic mass of matter; what it should be, you could not guess or define. It was entirely "without form and void; and darkness was upon the face of the deep." The Spirit came, and stretching his broad wings, bade the darkness disperse, and as he moved over it, all the different portions of matter came into their places, and it was no longer "without form, and void;" but became round, like its sister planets, and moved, singing the high praises of God—not discordantly, as it had done before, but as one great note in the vast scale of creation. Milton very beautifully describes this work of the Spirit, in thus bringing order out of confusion, when the King of Glory, in his powerful Word and Spirit, came to create new worlds:—

"On heavenly ground they stood; and from the shore
They viewed the vast, immeasurable abyss,
Outrageous as a sea, dark, wasteful, wild,
Up from the bottom turned by furious winds
And surging waves, as mountains, to assault
Heaven's height, and with the centre mix the pole.
"Silence, ye troubled waves, and thou deep, peace,
Said then the Omnific Word; your discord end.
Then on the watery calm,
His brooding wings the Spirit of God outspread
And vital virtue infused, and vital warmth
Throughout the fluid mass."

This you see, then, is the power of the Spirit. Could we have seen that earth all in confusion, we should have said, "Who can make a world out of this?" The answer would have been, "The power of the Spirit can do it. By the simple spreading of his dove-like wings, he can make all the things come together. Upon that there shall be order where there was naught but confusion." Nor is this all the power of the Spirit. We have seen some of his works in creation. But there was one particular instance of creation in which the Holy Spirit was more especially concerned; viz., the formation of the body of our Lord Jesus Christ. Though our Lord Jesus Christ was born of a woman, and made in the likeness of sinful flesh, yet, the power that begat him was entirely in God the Holy Spirit—as the Scriptures express it, "The Holy One of Israel shall overshadow thee." He was begotten, as the Apostles' Creed says, begotten of the Holy Ghost. "That holy thing which is born of thee shall be called the Son of the Highest." The corporeal frame of the Lord Jesus Christ was a master-piece of the Holy Spirit. I suppose his body to have excelled all others in beauty; to have been like that of the first man, the very pattern of what the body is to be in heaven, when it shall shine forth in all its glory. That fabric, in all its beauty and perfection, was modeled by the Spirit. "In his book were all the members written, when as yet there were none of them." He fashioned and formed him; and here again we have another instance of the creative energy of the Spirit.

2. A second manifestation of the Holy Spirit's power is to be found in the resurrection of the Lord Jesus Christ. If ye have ever studied this subject, ye have perhaps been rather perplexed to find that sometimes the resurrection of Christ is ascribed to himself. By his own power and godhead he could not be held by the bond of death, but as he willingly gave up his life he had power to take it up again. In another portion of Scripture, you find it ascribed to God the Father: "He raised him up from the dead:" "Him hath God the Father exalted." And many other passages of similar import. But, again, it is said in Scripture that Jesus Christ was raised by the Holy Spirit. Now, all these things were true. He was raised by the Father Because the Father said, "Loose the prisoner—let him go. Justice is satisfied. My law requires no more satisfaction—vengeance has had its due—let him go." Here he gave an official message which delivered Jesus from the grave. He was raised by his own majesty and power, because he had a right to come out; and he felt he had, and therefore "burst the bonds of death: he could be no longer holden of them." But he was raised by the Spirit as to that energy which his mortal

frame received, by the which it rose again from the grave after having lain there for three days and nights. If you want proofs of this you must open your Bibles again, 1 Peter 3:18. "For Christ also hath once suffered for sins, the just for the unjust, that he might bring us to God, being put to death in the flesh but quickened by the Spirit." And a further proof you may find in Romans 8:11—(I love sometimes to be textual, for I believe the great fault of Christians is that they do not search the Scriptures enough, and I will make them search them when they are here if they do not do so anywhere else.) —"But if the Spirit of him that raised up Jesus from the dead dwell in you, he that raised up Christ from the dead shall also quicken your mortal bodies by his Spirit that dwelleth in you."

The resurrection of Christ, then, was effected by the agency of the Spirit! And here we have a noble illustration of his omnipotence. Could you have stepped, as angels did, into the grave of Jesus, and seen his sleeping body, you would have found it cold as any other corpse. Lift up the hand; it falls by the side. Look at the eye; it is glazed. And there is a death-thrust which must have annihilated life. See his hands: the blood distills not from them. They are cold and motionless. Can that body live? Can it start up? Yes; and be an illustration of the might of the Spirit. For when the power of the Spirit came on him, as it was when it fell upon the dry bones of the valley, "he arose in the majesty of his divinity, and, bright and shining, astonished the watchmen so that they fled away; yea, he arose no more to die, but to live forever, King of kings and Prince of the kings of the earth."

3. The third of the works of the Holy Spirit, which have so wonderfully demonstrated his power, are attestation works. I mean by this—works of witnessing. When Jesus Christ went into the stream of baptism in the river Jordan, the Holy Spirit descended upon him like a dove, and proclaimed him God's beloved son. That was what I style an attestation work. And when afterwards Jesus Christ raised the dead, when he healed the leper, when he spoke to diseases and they fled apace, when demons rushed in thousands from those who were possessed of them, it was done by the power of the Spirit. The Spirit dwelt in Jesus without measure, and by that power all those miracles were worked. These were attestation works. And when Jesus Christ was gone, you will remember that master attestation of the Spirit, when he came like a rushing mighty wind upon the assembled apostles, and cloven tongues sat upon them; and you will remember how he attested their ministry, by giving them to speak with tongues as he gave them utterance;

and how, also, miraculous deeds were wrought by them, how they taught, how Peter raised Dorcas, how he breathed life into Enticus, how great deeds were wrought by the apostles as well as their Master—so that "mighty signs and wonders were done by the Holy Ghost, and many believed thereby." Who will doubt the power of the Holy Spirit after that? Ah! Those Socinians who deny the existence of the Holy Ghost and his absolute personality, what will they do when we get them on creation, resurrection, and attestation? They must rush in the very teeth of Scripture. But mark! It is a stone upon which if any man fall he shall be bruised; but if it fall upon him, as it will do if he resists it, it shall grind him to powder. The Holy Spirit has power omnipotent, even the power of God.

4. Once more, if we want another outward and visible sign of the power of the Spirit, we may look at the works of grace. Behold a city where a soothsayer hath the power—who has given out himself to be some great one, a Philip enters it and preaches the Word of God; straightway a Simon Magus loses his power and himself seeks for the power of the Spirit to be given to him, fancying it might be purchased with money. See, in modern times, a country where the inhabitants live in miserable wigwams, feeding on reptiles and the meanest creatures; observe them bowing down before their idols and worshiping their false gods, and so plunged in superstition, so degraded and debased, that it became a question whether they had souls or not; behold a Moffat go with the Word of God in his hand, hear him preach as the Spirit gives him utterance, and accompanies that Word with power. They cast aside their idols—they hate and abhor their former lusts; they build houses, wherein they dwell; they become clothed, and in their right mind. They break the bow, and cut the spear in sunder; the uncivilized become civilized; the savage becomes polite; he who knew nothing begins to read the Scriptures: thus out of the mouths of Hottentots, God attests the power of his mighty Spirit. Take a household in this city—and we could guide you to many such —the father is a drunkard; he has been the most desperate of characters; see him in his madness, and you might just as well meet an unchained tiger as meet such a man. He seems as if he could rend a man to pieces who should offend him. Mark his wife. She, too, has a spirit in her, and when he treats her ill she can resist him; many broils have been seen in that house. And often has the neighborhood been disturbed by the noise created there. As for the poor little children—see them in their rags and nakedness, poor untaught things. Untaught, did I say? They are taught and well taught in the devil's

school, and are growing up to be the heirs of damnation. But some one whom God has blessed by his Spirit is guided to the house. He may be but an humble city missionary, perhaps, but he speaks to such a one: "Oh!" says he, "come and listen to the voice of God." Whether it is by his own agency, or a minister's preaching, the Word, which is quick and powerful, cuts to the sinner's heart. The tears run down his cheeks—such as had never been seen before. He shakes and quivers. The strong man bows down—the mighty man trembles—and those knees that never shook begin to knock together. That heart which never quailed before now begins to shake before the power of the Spirit. He sits down on an humble bench by the penitent; he lets his knees bend, whilst his lips utter a child's prayer; but, whilst a child's prayer, a prayer of a child of God. He becomes a changed character. Mark the reformation in his house! That wife of his becomes the decent matron. Those children are the credit of the house, and in due time they grow up like olive branches round his table, adorning his house like polished stones. Pass by the house—no noise or broils, but songs of Zion. See him—no drunken revelry; he has drained his last cup, and, now forswearing it, he comes to God and is his servant. Now, you will not hear at midnight the bacchanalian shout; but should there be a noise, it will be the sound of the solemn hymn of praise to God. And, now, is there not such a thing as the power of the Spirit? Yes! And those must have witnessed it, and seen it. I know a village, once perhaps the most profane in England—a village inundated by drunkenness and debauchery of the worst kind, where it was impossible almost for an honest traveler to stop in the public house without being annoyed by blasphemy; a place noted for incendiaries and robbers. One man, the ringleader of all, listened to the voice of God. That man's heart was broken. The whole gang came to hear the gospel preached, and they sat and seemed to reverence the preacher as if he were a God, and not a man. These men became changed and reformed; and every one who knows the place affirms that such a change had never been wrought but by the power of the Holy Ghost. Let the gospel be preached and the Spirit poured out, and you will see that it has such power to change the conscience, to ameliorate the conduct, to raise the debased, to chastise and to curb the wickedness of the race, that you must glory in it. I say, there is naught like the power of the Spirit. Only let that come, and, indeed, everything can be accomplished.

II. Now for the second point, THE INWARD AND SPIRITUAL POWER OF THE HOLY SPIRIT. What I have already spoken of may be seen; what I am about to speak of must be felt, and no man will apprehend what I say with truth unless he has felt it. The other, even the infidel must confess; the other, the greatest blasphemer cannot deny, if he speaks the truth; but this is what the one will laugh at as enthusiasm, and what the other will say is but the invention of our fevered fancies. However, we have a more sure word of testimony than all that they may say. We have a witness within. We know it is the truth, and we are not afraid to speak of the inward spiritual power of the Holy Ghost. Let us notice two or three things wherein the inward and spiritual power of the Holy Ghost is very greatly to be seen and extolled.

1. First, in that the Holy Ghost has a power over men's hearts. Now, men's hearts are very hard to affect. If you want to get at them for any worldly object, you can do it. A cheating world can win man's heart; a little gold can win man's heart; a trump of fame and a little clamor of applause can win man's heart. But there is not a minister breathing that can win man's heart himself. He can win his ears and make them listen; he can win his eyes, and fix those eyes upon him; he can win the attention, but the heart is very slippery. Yes! The heart is a fish that troubles all gospel fishermen to hold. You may sometimes pull it almost all out of the water; but, slimy as an eel, it slippeth between your fingers, and you have not captured it after all. Many a man has fancied that he has caught the heart, but has been disappointed. It would take a strong hunter to overtake the hart on the mountains. It is too fleet for human foot to approach. The Spirit alone has power over man's heart. Do you every try your power on a heart? If any man thinks that a minister can convert the soul, I wish he would try. Let him go and be a Sabbath School teacher. He shall take his class, he shall have the best books that can be obtained, he shall have the best rules, he shall draw his lines of circumvallation about his spiritual Sebastopol, he shall take the best boy in his class, and if he is not tired in a week I shall be very much mistaken. Let him spend four or five Sabbaths in trying; but he will say, "the young fellow is incorrigible." Let him try another. And he will have to try another, and another and another before he will manage to convert one. He will soon find "it is not by might nor power, but by my Spirit, saith the Lord." Can a minister convert? Can he touch the heart? David said, "Your hearts are as fat as grease." Aye, that is quite true; and we cannot get through so much grease at all. Our sword cannot get at the heart, it is encased in so much fatness; it is harder than a nether millstone. Many a good old Jerusalem blade has been blunted against the hard heart. Many a piece of the true steel that God has put

into the hand of his servants has had the edge turned by being set up against the sinner's heart. We cannot reach the soul, but the Holy Spirit can. "My beloved can put in his hand by the hole in the door, and my bowels will move for sin." He can give a sense of blood-bought pardon that shall dissolve a heart of stone. He can

"Speak with that voice which wakes the dead
And bids the sinner rise;
And makes the guilty conscience dread
The death that never dies."

He can make Sinai's thunders audible; yea, and he can make the sweet whisperings of Calvary enter into the soul. He has power over the heart of man. And here is a glorious proof of the omnipotence of the Spirit that he has rule over the heart.

   2. But if there is one thing more stubborn than the heart, it is the will. "My lord Will-be-will," as Bunyan calls him in his "Holy War," is a fellow who will not easily be bent. The will, especially in some men, is a very stubborn thing; and in all men, if the will is once stirred up to opposition, there is nothing can be done with them. Free-will somebody believes in. Free-will many dream of. Free-will! Wherever is that to be found? Once there was Free-will in Paradise, and a terrible mess Free-will made there; for it spoiled all Paradise and turned Adam out of the garden. Free-will was once in heaven; but it turned the glorious archangel out, and a third part of the stars of heaven fell into the abyss. I want nothing to do with Free-will, but I will try to see whether I have got a Free-will within. And I find I have. Very free will to evil but very poor will to that which is good. Free-will enough when I sin, but when I would do good, evil is present with me, and how to do that which I would I find not. Yet some boast of Free-will. I wonder whether those who believe in it have any more power over persons' wills than I have? I know I have not any. I find the old proverb very true, "One man can bring a horse to the water but a hundred cannot make him drink." I find that I can bring you all to the water, and a great many more than can get into this chapel; but I cannot make you drink; and I don't think a hundred ministers could make you drink. I have read old Rowland Hill, and Whitefield, and several others, to see what they did; but I cannot discover a plan of turning your will. I cannot coax you, and you will not yield by any manner of means. I do not think any man has power over his fellow-creature's will, but the Spirit of God has. "I will make them willing in the day of my power." He

135

maketh the unwilling sinner so willing that he is impetuous after the gospel; he who was obstinate now hurries to the cross. He who laughed at Jesus now hangs on his mercy; and he who would not believe is now made by the Holy Spirit to do it, not only willingly, but eagerly; he is happy, is glad to do it, rejoices in the sound of Jesus' name, and delights to run in the way of God's commandments. The Holy Spirit has power over the will.

3. And yet there is one thing more which I think is rather worse than the will. You will guess what I mean. The will is somewhat worse than the heart to bend, but there is one thing that excels the will in its naughtiness, and that is the imagination. I hope that my will is managed by Divine Grace. But I am afraid my imagination is not at times. Those who have a fair share of imagination know what a difficult thing it is to control. You cannot restrain it. It will break the reins. You will never be able to manage it. The imagination will sometimes fly up to God with such a power that eagles' wings cannot match it. It sometimes has such might that it can almost see the King in his beauty, and the land which is very far off. With regard to myself, my imagination will sometimes take me over the gates of iron, across the infinite unknown, to the very gates of pearl, and discover the blessed glorified. But, if it is potent one way, it is another: for my imagination has taken me down to the vilest kennels and sewers of earth. It has given me thoughts so dreadful, that, while I could not avoid them, yet I was thoroughly horrified at them. These thoughts will come; and when I feel in the holiest frame, the most devoted to God, and the most earnest in prayer, it often happens that that is the very time when the plague breaks out the worst. But I rejoice and think of one thing, that I can cry out when this imagination comes upon me. I know it is said in the Book of Leviticus, when an act of evil was committed, if the maiden cried out against it, then her life was to be spared. So it is with the Christian. If he cries out, there is hope. Can you chain your imagination? No; but the power of the Holy Ghost can. Ah, it shall do it! And it does do it at last, it does it even on earth.

III. But the last thing was, THE FUTURE AND DESIRED EFFECTS; for, after all, though the Holy Spirit has done so much, he cannot say, "It is finished." Jesus Christ could exclaim concerning his own labor—"It is finished." But the Holy Spirit cannot say that. He has more to do yet: and until the consummation of all things, when the Son himself becomes subject to the Father, it shall not be said by the Holy Spirit, "It is finished." What, then, has the Holy Spirit to do?

1. First, he has to perfect us in holiness. There are two kinds of perfection which a Christian needs: one is the perfection of justification in the person of Jesus; and the other is, the perfection of sanctification worked in him by the Holy Spirit. At present corruption still rests even in the breasts of the regenerate. At present the heart is partially impure. At present there are still lusts and evil imaginations. But, oh! My soul rejoices to know that the day is coming when God shall finish the work which he has begun; and he shall present my soul, not only perfect in Christ, but perfect in the Spirit, without spot or blemish, or any such thing. And is it true that this poor depraved heart is to become as holy as that of God? And is it true that this poor spirit, which often cries, "O, wretched man that I am, who shall deliver me from the body of this sin an death!" shall get rid of sin and death? I shall have no evil things to vex my ears, and no unholy thoughts to disturb my peace. Oh happy hour! May it be hastened! Just before I die sanctification will be finished; but not till that moment shall I ever claim perfection in myself. But at that moment when I depart, my spirit shall have its last baptism in the Holy Spirit's fire. It shall be put in the crucible for its last trying in the furnace; and then, free from all dross, and fine, like a wedge of pure gold, it shall be presented at the feet of God without the least degree of dross or mixture. O glorious hour! O blessed moment! Methinks I long to die if there were no heaven, if I might but have that last purification come up from Jordan's stream most white from the washing. Oh! To be washed white, clean, pure, perfect! Not an angel more pure than I shall be—yea, not God himself more holy! And I shall be able to say, in a double sense, "Great God, I am clean—through Jesus' blood I am clean, through the Spirit's work I am clean too!" Must you not extol the power of the Holy Ghost in thus making us fit to stand before our Father in heaven?

2. Another great work of the Holy Spirit, which is not accomplished, is the bringing on of the latter-day glory. In a few more years—I know not when, I know not how—the Holy Spirit will be poured out in a far different style from the present. There are diversities of operations; and during the last few years it has been the case that the diversified operations have consisted in very little pouring out of the Spirit. Ministers have gone on in dull routine, continually preaching—preaching—preaching, and little good has been done. I do hope that perhaps a fresh era has dawned upon us, and that there is a better pouring out of the Spirit even now. For the hour is coming, and it may be even now is, when the Holy Ghost shall be poured out again in such

a wonderful manner, that many shall run to and fro, and knowledge shall be increased—the knowledge of the Lord shall cover the earth as the waters cover the surface of the great deep; when his kingdom shall come, and his will shall be done on earth even as it is in heaven. We are not going to be dragging on forever like Pharoah, with the wheels off his chariot. My heart exults, and my eyes flash with the thought that very likely I shall live to see the outpouring of the Spirit; when "the sons and the daughters of God again shall prophesy, and the young men shall see visions and the old men shall dream dreams." Perhaps there shall be no miraculous gifts—for they will not be required; but yet there shall be such a miraculous amount of holiness, such an extraordinary fervor of prayer, such a real communion with God, and so much vital religion, and such a spread of the doctrines of the cross, that every one will see that verily the Spirit is poured out like water, and the rains are descending from above. For that let us pray; let us continually labor for it, and seek it of God.

3. One more work of the Spirit, which will especially manifest his power—the general resurrection. We have reason to believe from Scripture, that the resurrection of the dead, whilst it will be effected by the voice of God and of his Word(the Son), shall also be brought about by the Spirit. The same power which raised Jesus Christ from the dead, shall also quicken your mortal bodies. The power of the resurrection is, perhaps, one of the finest proofs of the works of the Spirit. Ah! My friends, if this earth could but have its mantle torn away for a little while, if the green sod could be cut from it, and we could look about six feet deep into its bowels, what a world it would seem! What should we see? Bones, carcasses, rottenness, worms, corruption. And you would say, Can these dry bones live? Can they start up? Yes! "In a moment! In the twinkling of an eye, at the last trump, the dead shall be raised." He speaks; they are alive! See them scattered! Bone comes to his bone! See them naked; flesh comes upon them! See them still lifeless; "Come from the four winds, O breath, and breathe upon these slain!" When the wind of the Holy Spirit comes, they live; and they stand upon their feet an exceeding great army.

I have thus attempted to speak of the power of the Spirit, and I trust I have shown it to you. We must now have a moment or two for practical inference. The Spirit is very powerful, Christian! What do you infer from that fact? Why, that you never need distrust the power of God to carry you to heaven. O how that sweet verse was laid to my soul yesterday!

"His tried Almighty arm
is raised for your defense;
Where is the power can reach you there?
Or what can pluck you thence?"

The power of the Holy Spirit is your bulwark, and all his omnipotence defends you. Can your enemies overcome omnipotence? Then they can conquer you. Can they wrestle with Deity, and hurl him to the ground? Then they might conquer you. For the power of the Spirit is our power; the power of the Spirit is our might.

Once again, Christians, if this is the power of the Spirit, why should you doubt anything? There is your son. There is that wife of yours, for whom you have supplicated so frequently; do not doubt the Spirit's power. "Though he tarry, wait for him." There is thy husband, O holy woman! And thou hast wrestled for his soul. And though he is ever so hardened and desperate a wretch, and treats thee ill, there is power in the Spirit. And, O ye who have come from barren churches, with scarcely a leaf upon the tree, do not doubt the power of the Spirit to raise you up. For it shall be a "pasture for flocks, a den of wild asses," open but deserted, until the Spirit is poured out from on high. And then the parched ground shall be made a pool, and the thirsty land springs of water; and in the habitations of dragons, where each lay shall be grass with reeds and rushes. And, O ye members of Park Street! Ye who remember what your God has done for you especially, never distrust the power of the Spirit. Ye have seen the wilderness blossom like Carmel, ye have seen the desert blossom like the rose, trust him for the future. Then go out and labor with this conviction, that the power of the Holy Ghost is able to do anything. Go to your missionary enterprise; go to your preaching in your rooms, with the conviction that the power of the Spirit is our great help.

And now, lastly, to you sinners:—What is there to be said to you about this power of the Spirit? Why, to me, there is some hope for some of you. I cannot save you; I cannot get at you. I make you cry sometimes—you wipe your eyes, and it is all over. But I know my Master can. That is my consolation. Chief of sinners, there is hope for thee! This power can save you as well as anybody else. It is able to break your heart, though it is an iron one; to make your eyes run with tears, though they have been like rocks before. His power is able this morning, if he will, to change your heart, to turn the current of all your ideas; to make you at once a child of God, to justify you in Christ. There is power enough in the Holy Spirit. Ye are not straightened in him, but in your own bowels. He is able to bring sinners to Jesus; he is able to make you willing in the day of his power. Are you willing this morning? Has he gone so far as to make you desire his name; to make you wish for Jesus? Then, O sinner! Whilst he draws you, say, "Draw me, I am wretched without thee." Follow him, follow him; and, while he leads, tread you in his footsteps, and rejoice that he has begun a good work in you, for there is an evidence that he will continue it even unto the end. And, O desponding one! Put thy trust in the power of the Spirit. Rest on the blood of Jesus, and thy soul is safe, not only now, but throughout eternity. God bless you, my hearers. Amen.

Chapter 11
THE OUTPOURING OF THE HOLY SPIRIT

"While Peter yet spake these words, the Holy Ghost fell on all them which heard the Word"—Acts 10:44.

The Bible is a book of the Revelation of God. The God after whom the heathen blindly searched, and for whom reason gropes in darkness, is here plainly revealed to us in the pages of divine authorship, so that he who is willing to understand as much of Godhead as man can know, may here learn it if he be not willingly ignorant and wilfully obstinate. The doctrine of the Trinity is specially taught in Holy Scripture. The word certainly does not occur, but the three divine persons of the One God are frequently and constantly mentioned, and Holy Scripture is exceedingly careful that we should all receive and believe that great truth of the Christian religion, that the Father is God, that the Son is God, that the Spirit is God, and yet there are not three Gods but one God: though they be each of them very God of very God, yet three in one and one in three is the Jehovah whom we worship. You will notice in the works of Creation how carefully the Scriptures assure us that all the three divine persons took their share. "In the beginning Jehovah created the heavens and the earth;" and in another place we are told that God said "Let us make man"—not one person, but all three taking counsel with each other with regard to the making of mankind. We know that the Father hath laid the foundations and fixed those solid beams of light on which the blue arches of the sky are sustained; but we know with equal certainty that Jesus Christ, the eternal Logos, was with the Father in the beginning, and "without him was not anything made that was made:" moreover we have equal certainty that the Holy Spirit had a hand in Creation, for we are told that "the earth was without form and void, and darkness was upon the face of the earth; and the spirit of the Lord moved upon the face of the waters;" and brooding with his dove-like wing, he brought out of the egg of chaos this mighty thing, the fair round world. We have the like proof of the three persons in the Godhead in the matter of

Salvation. We know that God the, Father gave his Son; we have abundant proof that God the Father chose his people from before the foundations of the world, that he did invent the plan of salvation, and hath always given his free, willing, and joyous consent to the salvation of his people. With regard to the share that the Son had in salvation, that is apparent enough to all. For us men and for our salvation he came down from heaven; he was incarnate in a mortal body; he was crucified, dead, and buried; he descended into hades; the third day he rose again from the dead; he ascended into heaven; he sitteth at the right hand of God, where also he maketh intercession for us. As to the Holy Spirit, we have equally sure proof that the Spirit of God worketh in conversion; for everywhere we are said to be begotten of the Holy Spirit; continually it is declared, that unless a man be born again from above, he cannot see the kingdom of God; while all the virtues and the graces of Christianity are described as being the fruits of the Spirit, because the Holy Spirit doth from first to last work in us and carry out that which Jesus Christ hath beforehand worked for us in his great redemption, which also God the Father hath designed for us in his great predestinating scheme of salvation.

Now, it is to the work of the Holy Spirit that I shall this morning specially direct your attention; and I may as well mention the reason why I do so. It is this. We have received continually fresh confirmations of the good news from a far country, which has already made glad the hearts of many of God's people. In the United States of America there is certainly a great awakening. No sane man living there could think of denying it. There may be something of spurious excitement mixed up with it, but that good, lasting good, has been accomplished, no rational man can deny. Two hundred and fifty thousand persons—that is a quarter of a million—profess to have been regenerated since December last, have made a profession of their faith, and have united themselves with different sections of God's church. The work still progresses, if anything, at a more rapid rate than before, and that which makes me believe the work to be genuine is just this—that the enemies of Christ's holy gospel are exceedingly wroth at it. When the devil roars at anything, you may rest assured there is some good in it. The devil is not like some dogs we know of; he never barks unless there is something to bark at. When Satan howls we may rest assured he is afraid his kingdom is in danger. Now this great work in America has been manifestly caused by the outpouring of the Spirit, for no one minister has been a leader in it. All the ministers of the gospel have co-operated in it, but none of them have stood in the van. God himself has been the leader of his own hosts. It began with a desire for prayer. God's people began to pray; the prayer-meetings were better attended than before. it was then proposed to hold meetings at times that had never been set apart for prayer; these also were well attended; and now, in the city of Philadelphia, at the hour of noon, every day in the week, three thousand persons can always be seen assembled together for prayer in one place. Men of business, in the midst of their toil and labor, find an opportunity of running in there and offering a word of prayer, and then return to their occupations. And so, throughout all the States, prayer-meetings, larger or smaller in number, have been convened. And there has been real prayer. Sinners beyond all count, have risen up in the prayer-meeting, and have requested the people of God to pray for them; thus making public to the world that they had a desire after Christ; they have been prayed for, and the church has seen that God verily doth hear and answer prayer. I find that the Unitarian ministers for a little while took no notice of it. Theodore Parker snarls and raves tremendously at it, but he is evidently in a maze; he does not understand the mystery, and acts with regard to it as swine are said to do with pearls. While the church was found asleep, and doing very little, the Socinian could afford to stand in his pulpit and sneer at anything like evangelical religion, but now that there has been an awakening, he looks like a man that has just awakened out of sleep. He sees something; he does not know what it is. The power of religion is just that which will always puzzle the Unitarian, for he knows but little about that. At the form of religion he is not much amazed, for he can to an extent endorse that himself, but the supernaturalism of the gospel—the mystery—the miracle—the power—the demonstration of the Spirit that comes with the preaching, is what such men cannot comprehend, and they gaze and wonder, and then become filled with wrath, but still they have to confess there is something there they cannot understand, a mental phenomenon that is far beyond their philosophy—a thing which they cannot reach by all their science nor understand by all their reason.

   Now, if we have the like effect produced in this land, the one thing we must seek is the outpouring of the Holy Spirit, and I thought, perhaps, this morning in preaching upon the work of the Holy Spirit, that text might be fulfilled—"Him that honoureth me I will honor." My sincere desire is to honor the Holy Spirit this morning, and if he will be pleased to honor his church in return, unto him shall be the glory for ever.

"While Peter yet spake these words, the Holy Ghost fell on all them which heard the word." In the first place, I shall endeavor to describe the method of the Spirit's operation, secondly, the absolute necessity of the Holy Spirit's influence, if we could see men converted, and then, in the third place, I shall suggest the ways and means by which under divine grace we may obtain a like falling down of the Spirit upon our churches.

1. In the first place, then, I will endeavor to explain THE METHOD OF THE HOLY SPIRIT'S OPERATIONS. But let me guard myself against being misunderstood. We can explain what the Spirit does, but how he does it, no man must pretend to know. The work of the Holy Spirit is the peculiar mystery of the Christian religion. Almost any other thing is plain, but this must remain an inscrutable secret into which it were wrong for us to attempt to pry. Who knoweth where the winds are begotten? Who knoweth, therefore, how the Spirit worketh, for he is like the wind? "The wind bloweth where it listeth, and thou hearest the sound thereof but canst not tell whence it cometh, and whither it goeth: so is every one that is born of the Spirit." In Holy Scripture certain great secrets of nature are mentioned as being parallel with the secret working of the Spirit. The procreation of children is instanced as a parallel wonder, for we know not the mystery thereof; how much less, therefore, shall we expect to know that more secret and hidden mystery of the new birth and new creation of man in Christ Jesus. But let no man be staggered at this, for they are mysteries in nature: the wisest man will tell you there are depths in nature into which he cannot dive, and heights into which he cannot soar. He who pretends to have unravelled the knot of creation hath made a mistake, he may have cut the knot by his rough ignorance, and by his foolish conjectures, but the knot itself must remain beyond the power of man's unravelling, until God himself shall explain the secret. There are marvellous things, that, as yet, men have sought to know in vain. They may, perhaps, discover many of them, but how the Spirit works, no man can know. But now I wish to explain what the Holy Spirit does, although we cannot tell how he does it. I take it that the Holy Spirit's work in conversion is two-fold. First it is an awakening of the powers that man already has, and secondly, it is an implantation of powers which he never had at all.

In the great work of the new birth, the Holy Spirit first of all awakens the mental powers; for be it remembered that, the Holy Spirit never gives any man new mental powers. Take for instance reason—the Holy Spirit does not give men reason, for they have reason prior to their conversion. What the Holy Spirit does is to teach our reason, right reason—to set our reason in the right track, so that he can use it for the high purpose of discerning between good and evil; between the precious and vile. The Holy Spirit does not give man a will, for man has a will before; but he makes the will that was in bondage to Satan free to the service of God. The Holy Spirit gives no man the power to think, or the organ of belief—for man has power to believe or think as far as the mental act is concerned; but he gives that belief which is already there a tendency to believe the right thing, and he gives to the power of thought the propensity to think in the right way so that instead of thinking irregularly, we begin to think as God would have us think, and our mind desireth to walk in the steps of God's revealed truth There may be here, this morning, a man of enlarged understanding in things political—but his understanding is darkened with regard to spiritual things—he sees no beauty in the person of Christ—he sees nothing desirable in the way of holiness—he chooses the evil and forsakes the good. Now the Holy Spirit will not give him a new understanding, but he will cleanse his old understanding so that he will discern between things that differ, and shall discover that it is but a poor thing to enjoy "the pleasures of sin for a season," and let go an "eternal weight of glory." There shall be a man here too who is desperately set against religion, and willeth not to come to God, and do what we will, we are not able to persuade him to change his mind and turn to God. The Holy Spirit will not make a new will in that man, but he will turn his old will, and instead of willing to do evil he will make him will to do right—he will make him will to be saved by Christ—he will make him "willing in the day of his power." Remember, there is no power in man so fallen but that the Holy Spirit can raise it up. However debased a man may be, in one instant, by the miraculous power of the Spirit, all his faculties may be cleansed and purged. Ill-judging reason may be made to judge rightly; stout, obstinate wills may be made to run willingly in the ways of God's commandments; evil and depraved affections may in an instant be turned to Christ, and old desires that are tainted with vice, may be replaced by heavenly aspirations. The work of the Spirit on the mind is the re-modelling of it; the new forming of it. He doth not bring new material to the mind—it is in another part of the man that he puts up a new structure—but he puts the mind that had fallen out of order into its proper shape. He builds up pillars that had fallen down, and erects the palaces that had crumbled to the earth. This is the first work of the Holy

Spirit upon the mind of man.

Besides this, the Holy Spirit gives to men powers which they never had before. According to Scripture, I believe man is constituted in a three-fold manner. He has a body; by the Holy Spirit that body is made the temple of the Lord. He has a mind; by the Holy Spirit that mind is made like an altar in the temple. But man by nature is nothing higher than that; he is mere body and soul. When the Spirit comes, he breathes into him a third higher principle which we call the spirit. The apostle describes man as man, "body, soul and spirit." Now if you search all the mental writers through, you will find they all declare there are only two parts—body and mind; and they are quite right, for they deal with unregenerate man; but in regenerate man there is a third principle as much superior to mere mind as mind is superior to dead animal matter—that third principle is that with which a man prays; it is that with which he lovingly believes; or rather it is that which compels the mind to perform their acts. It is that which, operating upon the mind, makes the same use of the mind as the mind does of the body. When, after desiring to walk I make my legs move, it is my mind that compels them; and so my Spirit, when I desire to pray, compels my mind to think the thought of prayer and compels my soul also, if I desire to praise, to think the thought of praise, and lift itself upward towards God. As the body without the soul is dead, so the soul without the Spirit is dead, and one work of the Spirit is to quicken the dead soul by breathing into it the firing Spirit; as it is written, "The first man, Adam, was made a living soul, but the second Adam was made a quickening Spirit"—and, "as we have borne the image of the earthy, so must we bear the image of the heavenly;" that is, we must have in us, if we would be converted, the quickening Spirit, which is put into us by God the Holy Ghost. I say again, the spirit has powers which the mind never has. It has the power of communion with Christ, which to a degree is a mental act, but it can no more be performed by man without the Spirit, than the act of walking could be performed by man, if he were destitute of a soul to suggest the idea of walking. The Spirit suggests the thoughts of communion which the mind obeys and carries out. Nay, there are times, I think, when the spirit leaves the mind altogether, times when we forget everything of earth and one almost ceases to think, to reason, to judge, to weigh, or to will. Our souls are like the chariots of Amminadib, drawn swiftly onwards without any powers of volition. We lean upon the breast of Jesus, and in rhapsody divine, and in ecstasy celestial, we enjoy the fruits of the land of the blessed, and pluck the clusters of Eschol before entering into the land of promise.

I think I have clearly put these two points before you. The work of the Spirit consists, first, in awakening powers already possessed by man, but which were asleep and out of order; and in the next place in putting into man powers which he had not before. And to make this simple to the humblest mind, let me suppose man to be something like a machine; all the wheels are out of order, the cogs do not strike upon each other, the wheels do not turn regularly, the rods will not act, the order is gone. Now, the first work of the Spirit is to put these wheels in the right place, to fit the wheels upon the axles, to put the right axle to the right wheel, then to put wheel to wheel, so that they may act upon each other. But that is not all his work. The next thing is to put fire and steam so that these things shall go to work. He does not put fresh wheels, he puts old wheels into order, and then he puts the motive power which is to move the whole. First he puts our mental powers into their proper order and condition, and then he puts a living quickening spirit, so that all these shall move according to the holy will and law of God.

But, mark you, this is not all the Holy Spirit does. For if he were to do this, and then leave us, none of us would get to heaven. If any of you should be so near to heaven that you could hear the angels singing over the walls—if you could almost see within the pearly gates still, if the Holy Spirit did not help you the last step, you would never enter there. All the work is through his divine operation. Hence it is the Spirit who keeps the wheels in motion, and who tales away that defilement which, naturally engendered by our original sin, falls upon the machine and puts it out of order. He takes this away, and keeps the machine constantly going without injury, until at last he removes man from the place of defilement to the land of the blessed, a perfect creature, as perfect as he was when he came from the mould of his Maker.

And I must say, before I leave this point, that all the former part of what I have mentioned is done instantaneously. When a man is converted to God, it is done in a moment. Regeneration is an instantaneous work. Conversion to God, the fruit of regeneration, occupies all our life, but regeneration itself is effected in an instant. A man hates God; the Holy Spirit makes him love God. A man is opposed to Christ, he hates his gospel, does not understand it and will not receive it: the Holy Spirit comes, puts light into his darkened understanding, takes the chain from his bandaged will, gives liberty to his conscience, gives life to his dead soul, so that the voice of conscience is heard, and the man becomes a new creature in Christ Jesus. And all this is done, mark you, by the instantaneous supernatural influence of God the Holy Ghost working as he willeth among the sons of men.

II. Having thus dwelt upon the method of the Holy Spirit's work, I shall now turn to the second point, THE ABSOLUTE NECESSITY OF THE SPIRIT'S WORK IN ORDER TO CONVERSION. In our text we are told that "while Peter spake these words, the Holy Ghost fell on all them which heard the word." Beloved, the Holy Ghost fell on Peter first, or else it would not have fallen on his hearers. There is a necessity that the preacher himself, if we are to have souls saved, should be under the influence of the Spirit. I have constantly made it my prayer that I might be guided by the Spirit even in the smallest and least important parts of the service; for you cannot tell but that the salvation of a soul may depend upon the reading of a hymn, or upon the selection of a chapter. Two persons have joined our church and made a profession of being converted simply through my reading a hymn—
"Jesus, lover of my soul"
They did not remember anything else in the hymn, but those words made such a deep impression upon their mind, that they could not help repeating them for days afterwards, and then the thought arose, "Do I love Jesus?" And then they considered what strange ingratitude it was that he should be the lover of their souls, and yet they should not love him. Now I believe the Holy Spirit led me to read that hymn. And many persons have been converted by some striking saying of the preacher. But why was it the preacher uttered that saying? Simply because he was led thereunto by the Holy Spirit. Rest assured, beloved, that when any part of the sermon is blessed to your heart, the minister said it because he was ordered to say it by his Master. I might preach to-day a sermon which I preached on Friday, and which was useful then, and there might be no good whatever come from it now, because it might not be the sermon which the Holy Ghost would have delivered to-day. But if with sincerity of heart I have sought God's guidance in selecting the topic, and he rests upon me in the preaching of the Word, there is no fear but that it shall be found adapted to your immediate wants. The Holy Spirit must rest upon your preachers. Let them have all the learning of the wisest men, and all the eloquence of such men as Desmosthenes and Cicero, still the Word cannot be blessed to you, unless first of all the Spirit of God hath guided the minister's mind in the selection of his subject, and in the discussion of it.

But if Peter himself were under the hand of the Spirit, that would fail unless the Spirit of God, then, did fall upon our hearers; and I shall endeavor now to show the absolute necessity of the Spirit's work in the conversion of men.

Let us remember what kind of thing the work is, and we shall see that other means are altogether out of the question. It is quite certain that men cannot be converted by physical means. The Church of Rome thought that she could convert men by means of armies; so she invaded countries, and threatened them with war and bloodshed unless they would repent and embrace her religion. However, it availed but little, and men were prepared to die rather than leave their faith; she therefore tried those beautiful things—stakes, racks, dungeons, axes, swords, fire; and by these things she hoped to convert men. You have heard of the man who tried to wind up his watch with a pick-axe. That man was extremely wise, compared with the man who thought to touch mind through matter. All the machines you like to invent cannot touch mind. Talk about tying angel's wings with green withes, or manacling the cherubim with iron chains, and then talk about meddling with the minds of men through physical means. Why, the things don't set; they cannot act. All the king's armies that ever were, and all the warriors clothed with mail, with all their ammunition, could never touch the mind of man. That is an impregnable castle which is not to be reached by physical agency.

Nor, again, can man be converted by moral argument. "Well," says one, "I think he may. Let a minister preach earnestly, and he may persuade men to be converted." Ah! beloved, it is for want of knowing better that you say so. Melancthon thought so, but you know what he said after he tried it—"Old Adam is too strong for young Melancthon." So will every preacher find it, if he thinks his arguments can ever convert man. Let me give you a parallel case. Where is the logic that can persuade an Ethiopian to change his skin? By what argument can you induce a leopard to renounce his spots? Even so may he that is accustomed to do evil learn to do well. But if the Ethiopian's skin be changed it must be by a supernatural process. and if the leopard's spots be removed, he that made the leopard must do it. Even so is it with the heart of man. If sin were a thing ab extra and external, we could induce man to change it. For instance, you may induce a man to leave off drunkenness or swearing, because those things are not a part of his nature—he has added that vice to his original depravity. But the hidden evil at the heart is beyond all moralsuasion. I dare say a man might have enough argument to induce him to hang himself, but I am certain no argument will ever induce him to hang his sins, to hang his self-righteousness, and to come and humble himself at the foot of the cross; for the religion of Christ is so contrary to all the propensities of man, that it is like swimming against the stream to approach it, for the stream of man's will and man's desire is exactly the opposite of the religion of Jesus Christ. If you wanted a proof of that, at the lifting of my finger, there are thousands in this hall who would rise to prove it, for they would say, "I have found it so sir, in my experience; I hated religion as much as any men; I despised Christ, and his people, and I know not to this day how it is that I am what I am, unless it be the work of God." I have seen the tears run down a man's cheeks when he has come to me in order to be united to the church of Christ, and he has said, "Sir, I wonder how it is I am here to-day, if anyone had told me a year ago that I should think as I now think, and feel as I now feel, I should have called him a born fool for his pains; I used to say I never would be one of those canting Methodists, I liked to spend my Sunday in pleasure, and I did not see why I was to be cooping myself up in the house of God listening to a man talk. I pray, sir? No, not I. I said the best providence in all the world was a good strong pair of hands, and to take care of what you got. If any man talked to me about religion, why I would slam the door in his face, and pretty soon put him out; but the things that I loved then, I now hate, and the things that then I hated, now I love, I cannot do or say enough to show how total is the change that has been wrought in me. It must have been the work of God; it could not have been wrought by me, I feel assured; it must be some one greater than myself, who could thus turn my heart." I think these two things are proofs that we want something more than nature, and since physical agency will not do, and mere moral suasion will never accomplish it, that there must be an absolute necessity for the Holy Spirit.

But again, if you will just think a minute what the work is, you will soon see that none but God can accomplish it. In the Holy Scripture, conversion is often spoken of as being a new creation. If you talk about creating yourselves, I should feel obliged if you would create a fly first. Create a gnat, create a grain of sand, and when you have created that, you may talk about creating a new heart. Both are alike, impossible, for creation is the work of God. But still, if you could create a grain of dust, or create even a world, it would not be half the miracle, for you must first find a thing which has created itself. Could that be? Suppose you had no existence, how could you create yourself? Nothing cannot produce anything. Now, how can man re-create himself. A man cannot create himself into a new condition, when he has no being in that condition, but is, as yet, a thing that is not.

Then, again, the work of creation is said to be like the resurrection. "We are alive from the dead." Now, can the dead in the grave raise themselves. Let any minister who thinks he can convert souls, go and raise a corpse let him go and stand in one of the cemeteries, and bid the tombs open wide their mouths, and make room for those once buried there to awaken, and he will have to preach in vain. But if he could do it, that is not the miracle: it is for the dead to raise themselves, for an inaminate corpse to kindle in its own breast the spark of life anew. If the work be a resurrection, a creation, does it not strike you that it must be beyond the power of man? It must be wrought in him by no one less than God himself.

And there is yet one more consideration, and I shall have concluded this point. Beloved, even if man could save himself, I would have you recollect how averse he is to it? If we could make our hearers all willing, the battle would be accomplished. "Well," says one, "If I am willing to be saved, can I not be saved?" Assuredly you can, but the difficulty is, we cannot bring men to be willing. That shows, therefore, that there must be a constraint put upon their will. There must be an influence exerted upon them, which they have not in themselves, in order to make them willing in the day of God's power. And this is the glory of the Christian religion. The Christian religion has within its own bowels power to spread itself. We do not ask you to be willing first. We come and tell you the news, and we believe that the Spirit of God working with us, will make you willing. If the progress of the Christian religion depended upon the voluntary assent of mankind it would never go an inch further but because the Christian religion has within an omnipotent influence, constraining men to believe it, it is therefore that it is and must be triumphant, "till like a sea of glory it spreads from shore to shore."

III. Now I shall conclude by bringing one or two thoughts forward, with regard to WHAT MUST BE DONE AT THIS TIME IN ORDER TO BRING DOWN THE HOLY SPIRIT. It is quite certain, beloved, if the Holy Spirit willed to do it, that every man, woman, and child in this place might be converted now. If God, the Sovereign Judge of all, would be pleased now to send out his Spirit, every inhabitant of this million-peopled city might be brought at once to turn unto the living God. Without instrumentality, without the preacher, without books, without anything, God has it in his power to convert men. We have known persons about their business, not thinking about religion at all, who have had a thought injected into their heart, and that thought has been the prolific mother of a thousand meditations. and through these meditations they have been brought to Christ. Without the aid of the minister, the Holy Spirit has thus worked, and to-day he is not restrained. There may be some men, great in infidelity, staunch in opposition to the cross of Christ, but, without asking their consent, the Holy Spirit can pull down the strong man, and make the mighty man bow himself. For when we talk of the Omnipotent God, there is nothing too great for him to do. But, beloved, God has been pleased to put great honor upon instrumentality; he could work without it if he pleased but he does not do so. However, this is the first thought I want to give you; if you would have the Holy Spirit exert himself in our midst, you must first of all look to him and not to instrumentality. When Jesus Christ preached, there were very few converted under him, and the reason was, because the Holy Spirit was not abundantly poured forth. He had the Holy Spirit without measure himself, but on others the Holy Spirit was not as yet poured out. Jesus Christ said, "Greater works than these shall ye do because I go to my Father, in order to send the Holy Spirit;" and recollect that those few who were converted under Christ's ministry, were not converted by him, but by the Holy Spirit that rested upon him at that time. Jesus of Nazareth was anointed of the Holy Spirit. Now then, if Jesus Christ, the great founder of our religion, needed to be anointed of the Holy Spirit, how much more our ministers? And if God would always make the distinction even between his own Son as an instrument, and the Holy Spirit as the agent, how much more ought we to be careful to do that between poor puny men and the Holy Spirit? Never let us hear you say again, "So many persons were converted by So-and so." They were not. If converted they were not converted by man. Instrumentality is to be used, but the Spirit is to have the honor of it. Pay no more a superstitious reverence to man, think no more that God is tied to your plans, and to your agencies. Do not imagine that so many city missionaries, so much good will be done. Do not say, "So many preachers; so many sermons, so many souls saved." Do not say, "So many Bibles, so many tracts; so much good done." Not so, use these, but remember it is not in that proportion the blessing comes; it is, so much Holy Spirit, so many souls in-gathered.

And now another thought. If we would have the Spirit, beloved, we must each of us try to honor him. There are some chapels into which if you were to enter, you would never know there was a Holy Spirit. Mary Magdalen said of old, "They have taken away my Lord, and I know not where they have laid him," and the Christian might often say so, for there is nothing said about the Lord until they come to the end, and then there is just the benediction, or else you would not know that there were three persons in one God at all. Until our churches honor the Holy Spirit, we shall never see it abundantly manifested in our midst. Let the preacher always confess before he preaches that he relies upon the Holy Spirit. Let him burn his manuscript and depend upon the Holy Spirit. If the Spirit does not come to help him, let him be still and let the people go home and pray that the Spirit will help him next Sunday.

And do you also, in the use of all your agencies, always honor the Spirit? We often begin our religious meetings without prayer; it is all wrong. We must honor the Spirit; unless we put him first, he will never make crowns for us to wear. He will get victories, but he will have the honor of them, and if we do not give to him the honor, he will never give to us the privilege and success. And best of all, if you would have the Holy Spirit, let us meet together earnestly to pray for him. Remember, the Holy Spirit will not come to us as a church, unless we seek him. "For this thing will I be enquired of by the house of Israel to do it for them." We purpose during the coming week to hold meetings of special prayer, to supplicate for a revival of religion. On the Friday morning I opened the first prayer meeting at Trinity Chapel, Brixton; and, I think, at seven o'clock, we had as many as two hundred and fifty persons gathered together. It was a pleasant sight. During the hour, nine brethren prayed, one after the other; and I am sure there was the spirit of prayer there. Some persons present sent up their names, asking that we would offer special petitions for them; and I doubt not the prayers will be answered; At Park Street, on Monday morning, we shall have a prayer. meeting from eight to nine; then during the rest of the week there will be a prayer-meeting in the morning from seven to eight. On Monday evening we shall have the usual prayer-meeting at seven, when I hope there will be a large number attending. I find that my brother, Baptist Noel, has commenced morning and evening prayer-meetings, and they have done the same thing in Norwich and many provincial towns, where, without any pressure, the people are found willing to come. I certainly did not expect to see so many as two hundred and fifty persons at an early hour in the morning meet together for prayer. I believe it was a good sign The Lord hath put prayer into their hearts and therefore they were willing to come, "Prove me now here, saith the Lord of host., and see if I do not pour you out a blessing so that there shall not be room enough to receive it." Let us meet and pray, and if God doth not hear us, it will be the first time he has broken his promise. Come, let us go up to the sanctuary; let us meet together in the house of the Lord, and offer solemn supplication; and I say again, if the Lord doth not make bare his arm in the sight of all the people, it will be the reverse of all his previous actions, it will be the contrary of all his promises, and contradictory to himself. We have only to try him, and the result is certain. In dependence on his Spirit, if we only meet for prayer, the Lord shall bless us, and all the ends of the earth shall fear him. O Lord, lift up thyself because of thine enemies; pluck thy right hand out of thy bosom, O Lord our God, for Christ's sake, Amen.

THE END

Printed in Great Britain
by Amazon